In a world full of contended ideas a[...]
David Sunde has practiced the rhythms ne has thoughtfully
articulated in *Small-Batch Disciplemaking*. Not only have I
watched him practice it around me, but I am also a product
of it personally. The investments of time and intention have
affected my life significantly. It has changed the way I look at
my personal life, professional life, married life, and parenting.
Each rhythm invites God into those areas of your life in
renewed ways. Discipleship was intended to influence every
part of our lives, not just our Sunday mornings. *Small-Batch
Disciplemaking* gives you the chance to be discipled in a way
that affects every part of your life.

IRINI FAMBRO, PhD, MDiv, owner of Intelligent Leadership

We crave change! Not just theoretical change but real,
practical, life-altering change. There is no more powerful way
to awaken change within the church, within our souls, and
within our neighborhoods than the work of apprenticeship.
Dave Sunde has written a beautifully eloquent but practical
primer on how to apprentice ordinary Christians to become
change agents in the world. *Small-Batch Disciplemaking* is
bathed in the genuine relational and spiritual mechanics of
how to pass on the life of Christ to another. Get this resource
in your hands and in your heart—it can create ripple effects
that will change everything!

DAN WHITE JR., author of *Love Over Fear*, coauthor of
The Church as Movement

In this book, Dave Sunde puts his finger on what makes faith work (and what is missing in so many churches and ministries). Far too often, we've made Christianity a cognitive experience but not a life experience. We don't go deep because we don't practice. We believe but we don't apprentice. Be warned: If you heed the big ideas in this book, you will be transformed. I highly recommend it.

DR. TIM ELMORE, CEO and founder of Growing Leaders, author of *A New Kind of Diversity*, coauthor of *Generation Z Unfiltered*

Want to grow in your faith? Want to help others do the same but don't know where to start? Then *Small-Batch Disciplemaking* is just what you need! I've known David Sunde for over twenty-five years, and I'm thrilled he is finally sharing his insights and experiences with the world! This field guide will be a resource you look to again and again as you journey with Jesus and help others do the same.

KURT JOHNSTON, pastor of NextGen Ministries at Saddleback Church

Sunde's book is a breath of fresh air. It walks alongside us, showing us a better way. The Western church is obsessed with numbers and programs, but Dave helps us see the importance of really doing life together. I mean, really. No performance. No lights. No show. Just simply what it looks like to follow Jesus together. Dave is the right person to write this book as it is the life he leads, the way he is. I highly recommend this book and the helpful brilliance in its pages.

TYRONE WELLS, recording artist with over 60 million Spotify streams and a #1 singer-songwriter album on iTunes

Small-Batch Disciplemaking calls us to reground ourselves in the ancient tenets of our faith, not in the sense of abstract theology but in core practices of transformational living. This writing is infused with the wisdom hard-won from his years of experience as a follower of Jesus and as a guide to many seeking to do the same. This book is a much-needed practical guide and theology of the church reimagined around the core practices of our faith. If you hunger for more in your spiritual life, this is a must-read.

Small-Batch Disciplemaking is a fresh and much-needed contribution to the practice of discipleship. This is a field manual that comes from David's effective ministry of discipling others. I've known David for many years. Discipleship is his passion, and this book is his legacy. After fifty plus years of leading churches, my assessment is that life-changing discipleship is the church's greatest weakness. We need this book!

Small-Batch Disciplemaking serves the church a large portion of wisdom that lays down a compelling baseline for a healthier twenty-first-century church. Dave Sunde identifies seven transferable rhythms that empower every Christian to fulfill their God-given responsibility: Make disciples!

A NavPress resource published in alliance
with Tyndale House Publishers

SMALL-BATCH DISCIPLEMAKING

A RHYTHM FOR TRAINING THE FEW TO REACH THE MANY

DAVID SUNDE

NavPress.com

Small-Batch Disciplemaking: A Rhythm for Training the Few to Reach the Many

Copyright © 2024 by David Sunde. All rights reserved.

A NavPress resource published in alliance with Tyndale House Publishers

NavPress and the NavPress logo are registered trademarks of NavPress, The Navigators, Colorado Springs, CO. *Tyndale* is a registered trademark of Tyndale House Ministries. Absence of ® in connection with marks of NavPress or other parties does not indicate an absence of registration of those marks.

The Team:
David Zimmerman, Publisher; Deborah Sáenz Gonzalez, Acquisitions Editor; Elizabeth Schroll, Copy Editor; Olivia Eldredge, Operations Manager; Libby Dykstra, Designer

Cover illustration of honey and spoons by Libby Dykstra. Copyright © Tyndale House Ministries. All rights reserved.

Interior illustration of bowl icon copyright © Resty Agnesia/TheNounProject.com. All rights reserved.

Author photo copyright © 2023 by Suzanne Covert Photography. All rights reserved.

The author is represented by the literary agency of WordServe Literary, www.wordserveliterary.com.

Some of the anecdotal illustrations in this book are true to life and are included with the permission of the persons involved. All other illustrations are composites of real situations, and any resemblance to people living or dead is purely coincidental.

For information about special discounts for bulk purchases, please contact Tyndale House Publishers at csresponse@tyndale.com, or call 1-855-277-9400.

ISBN 978-1-64158-813-3

Printed in the United States of America

30	29	28	27	26	25	24
7	6	5	4	3	2	1

TO TIM ELMORE, *who invited me to follow, helped me find my voice, and inspired me to invest my life in others.*

TO BIC MOORE, *who inspired me to become an elder. You showed me how to grow up without growing old. Even after three careers, you never retired from the Kingdom of heaven because you knew eternity had already begun.*

CONTENTS

FOREWORD

I REMEMBER THE FIRST TIME, years ago, when I heard David Sunde say, "Maybe *practice* is the new *deep*." Like an earworm that adhered itself to my brain cells, the idea wouldn't leave me. It kept rolling around in my mind, continuously occupying my thoughts, and I knew that the truth embedded in those words was worthy of my attention.

Those words countered the constant call of church members saying "I want to go deep!" . . . when there was little evidence of transformation coming from what they already knew. (I include myself in that chorus.)

How dangerous that we can so easily mistake information for transformation.

There is a comfort in the accumulation of knowledge, sound bites, and pieces of information I can use to convince myself that I live in the world of "deep." It builds a fortress around my soul, protecting the most vulnerable places from the hard work of change. It allows me to avoid facing the difficult things necessary for transformation to happen and puts me in just enough of a perceived superior position that I start to believe my own delusion.

I'd prefer to read another verse, even another chapter, than to have to sit for more than a minute in my pain, much less sit and ask the hard *Why?* questions. Give me another book to read or webinar to attend, but please don't ask me to practice moving toward someone I really don't like or to inconvenience myself for someone else or to admit that I have so many sins and give them names.

This book reminds us that there is a way, the way of Jesus . . . and it is not easy, but it is good. It does not exist in the clean lines of information but in the messy places of being and of making disciples throughout our lives. And so we practice. We think it over, write it down, and talk it through. We allow the words and ways of Jesus to capture our hearts, souls, and minds. We wrestle, we object, we submit, we question. We do it alone and in community. We practice our way toward living as disciples.

Dallas Willard often said that the way we spend our time reflects what we most deeply believe. What you are about to read will challenge and encourage you to spend your time on what really matters in ways that will allow you to grow old well with God. David has always had a way of using fresh language—words that take you by surprise, causing you to look at something you were so sure of from a new perspective. He brings a point of view that causes you to shift your thinking in ways that bring the truth into sharper focus. And how we need that.

Drawing on profound spiritual analogies, this book is a

winsome portal into the life of becoming the people we long to be. *Small-Batch Disciplemaking* offers a way to integrate faith and practice to know and see God more clearly, pulling us back to the way of Jesus that is personal, tailored, and developmental. Rhythms of planting, cultivating, waiting, and reaping remind us of the time factor, which I am so hopelessly impatient with. Jesus often used the phrases *you have heard it said . . . but I tell you . . .* to guide us into the unlearning that is necessary to follow God well. That's the needed approach that fills this book. So turn the page with expectation. I did, and I was not disappointed.

Nancy Ortberg
CEO of Transforming the Bay
with Christ

INTRODUCTION

Disciples Aren't Mass-Produced

HAVE YOU EVER THOUGHT about the difference between an inheritance and a legacy? The words are often used interchangeably. Both suggest something of value is left behind after a person's life on earth is over. But there's one notable distinction.

An inheritance is something we leave for *someone.*
A legacy is what we leave in *them.*

There are things that my children will inherit from my wife and me. Some are items of worth. Others are sentimental. All will have some value, at least to our kids, because of the life we share. However, the deposits we will leave *in* them are more enduring. Things like practicing peacemaking and reconciling relationships, demonstrating trust in God as the Source by stewarding personal resources and hospitality in Jesus' name, crossing social divides in support of fellow image bearers of God, and prioritizing faith and community with a standing appointment that's not crowded out by kids' sports, birthday parties, and home-improvement projects. All these deposits reveal where we place our hope. Simply put, a living hope begins with a living faith!

When it comes to leaving a spiritual legacy, our influence extends beyond our children. There are many people whom I care about deeply who won't inherit a thing from me. But because of the resurrection of Jesus and the faith experiences that I have had throughout my life, I want to steward my influence in such a way that people experience the reality of God's redeeming love—long after I'm gone. What if we Christians began seeing our faith as a legacy-building endeavor whereby our primary mission is passing on a living faith and hope to those with whom we have influence?

As with parents leaving a legacy for their children, Christians should seek to make spiritual investments in the lives of those closest to us. When it comes to our pursuits, sometimes we follow with reckless abandon and passion. Other times we follow obediently or even out of obligation. Parenting is one of the most humbling pursuits. But it can also be the most formative, if we let it. It's hard to feel prepared, confident, or poised for what parenting throws your way. The same can be said of stewarding your faith. There's always more to learn and room to grow, so much so that it too often paralyzes earnest followers of Jesus from investing in the spiritual development of others.

But what is belief without action? And while we'll always feel like a spiritual work in progress, the great legacy question is *What can we do with what we have already experienced, learned, and overcome?*

This question is more pressing than ever. Our society's primary institutions have left an unfortunate legacy of a lack of credibility. Government, marriage, family, education, and even the church are hardly viewed today as trustworthy or effective in leading, much less supportive. We've seen the nuclear family crumble with marriage commitments increasingly based on feeling happy rather than as a laboratory for God to help us become holy. Resistance to government has exploded in even the most democratic settings. Religious ties have weakened, with a growing number of people spiritually curious but institutionally skeptical. And many churches are more invested in preserving and expanding their facilities than in being a social enterprise for God's redemptive plan.

This last point is particularly troubling for anyone who feels compelled to steward and pass on a living faith. In *The Church as Movement*, JR Woodward and Dan White Jr. describe the church as a "Christian-industrial complex," both an apt and an unfortunate description of many churches.[1] We've chosen growth in size over growth in disciplemaking. Buildings get built, staff are added, and then instead of sending people out to live life on mission, we need people to return and help support the overhead. To grow ministries, we launch scalable programs to funnel believers into. This isn't bad in and of itself, but it has a way of mainly producing religious consumption. And the thing we all want—for faith in a living God to change people from the inside out—doesn't occur in consumers. The disciplemaking mission doesn't gain much-needed traction as Christians bounce around between churches for religious goods and services. And yet it is this work—the slow, relationship-driven craft of small-batch disciplemaking—to which God has called us.

HANDCRAFTING A SPIRITUAL LEGACY

The words *follow me* loom large. Not because I read them in one of the Gospels but because I embraced them as an invitation. When I was twenty-two years old, my college pastor, Tim Elmore, asked if I wanted to be discipled. Having grown up in church, I associated that word with Sunday school, Bible study, and Scripture memorization. "Being discipled" sounded intense, like a church without fellowship.

This was not that.

Tim's invitation to discipleship was a chance to follow him closely and purposefully. It meant my being coached as much as our studying together. I was to become an apprentice, which meant there was as much "laboratory" time as there was "lecture" time. It was the experiment to the theory. As I began apprenticing with Tim, he laid the groundwork, saying, "Dave, you seem to already have a good basis in knowing Christ. I don't want to teach you anything new. I just want to make sure you know how to give away what you know." No longer was my walk with God about me being saved or about going to heaven when I die, as if faith were a personal insurance policy. It was about a living faith that would align more people with life in Christ.

Then Tim said these unforgettable words, which are contrary

to how most church structures operate: "More time with fewer people equals greater Kingdom impact!" This shift opened my eyes to the present reality of God's Kingdom on earth, here and now. But it also helped me realize that Jesus' original intent for making disciples—the ordinary Christian life—meant spiritual reproduction. I wouldn't be the first to suggest that the church doesn't have a mission. Instead, the mission has a church: Make disciples.[2]

A disciple is one who, rooted in the love of Christ, (1) develops an ability to talk about personal faith; (2) grows an intentional spiritual practice; and (3) stewards and shares it with those closest to them. What if that basic definition became the everyday Christian life?

As we've noted, there's a systemic problem in how we've approached God's mission to make disciples. Truthfully, the church should look like a sending agent rather than a place to grow old and safe. We have a discipleship crisis primarily due to a one-size-fits-all, mass-produced approach to Christian education. When it comes to church, we mustn't confuse the vision with the vehicle. Too often, people (leaders especially) baptize a way of doing church and lose sight of the vision. *Well, we need to teach the Word of God*, the thinking goes, *so therefore, we need a weekly teaching event*. But who does that study benefit most? The pastor or other speaker. What are some other ways to deliver vital content?

According to Barna Research, "one in four [Christians] says the practice of discipling others hasn't been suggested to them (24%) or they haven't thought about helping someone grow closer to God (22%)."[3] That's a problem. But to solve it, what's needed isn't more creative Bible teaching or higher-quality services but a more effective way to integrate faith into life. We need simple faith expressions that reflect the heart of God personally. We need practices that form Christ in us and leverage our faith for others' benefit. We need practices, or rhythms, to impart a living faith—in word and deed—to those closest to us. Simply put, *disciples aren't mass-produced.*

The disciplemaking process was never supposed to happen en masse. Spiritual formation doesn't happen by singing songs, observing Communion, and listening to biblical teaching. But that's how we do church: one size fits all. My passion is to help Christians see that disciplemaking in small batches is the most effective way to live into our calling. We must learn how to train the few to reach the many.

Every generation holds a sacred trust to pass the baton of the transforming work of Christ to the next generation. Of course, the greatest witness of this testimony is found when individual disciples learn to talk about the difference Christ is making in them. I like to think this is what Jesus had in mind when He sent out the disciples in Luke 10 and told them to proclaim the Kingdom of God (Luke 10:9; also see Matthew 10:7). The greatest challenge facing Christianity today isn't persecution, political correctness, or scandals from within the church; too many believers give mental assent to basic Christian tenets without reorienting their life to prioritize life in Christ.

HOW A TRANSFORMATIONAL PROCESS WORKS

What if you could develop a new practice of small-batch disciplemaking through regular but thoughtful expressions of faith? Rather than funneling people through the church, what if you invested in their growth—and then lived out your faith *together in community*? This kind of intentional investment could help you discover a new kind of Christian purpose and spiritual legacy.

That's where the rhythm dynamics of this book come in. By faith, we move upward through rhythms of generosity, gratitude, and renewal. We strengthen the church body by practicing rhythms of community and apprenticing. And we grow outwardly, as missional practitioners, through rhythms of hospitality and compassion. When a significant event occurs or a life change happens, we tend to try to repeat the experience. We want to create a formula when, in fact, transformation is much more organic and unique than scalable. It's specific to individuals, unlike a one-size-fits-all process. There are things we can do, however, to make the soil fertile for impact and transformation. We could benefit from practical expressions of faith so that our hearts and lives might be further formed into the image of the living God!

It's not enough to just talk about our faith or celebrate having a similar belief as someone else. Spiritual growth is more than simply gaining information. These rhythms are a way of unifying a congregation so that we can *be* the church whether we're gathered or scattered throughout the week. It's a way to not only be a disciple but also become a disciplemaker.

The rhythms outlined here are not impactful by themselves; the truth is, many things contribute to one's spiritual formation. But they provide an intentional way to experience God's direction and desires. They offer ways to experience the Kingdom of God at work. Whether we are on the giving or receiving end of a disciplemaking relationship, these rhythms give the Holy Spirit room to mold, expand, refine, and echo a living faith. Because it's a process, the change will never feel like winning the lottery, where one day you are suddenly rich. Instead, transformation is more like an alcoholic practicing sobriety daily for twenty years—they still live with tension and temptation each day. It's the same with us as we give our hearts to being formed into the image and righteousness of Christ Jesus. These rhythms offer a practical way to pursue a changed heart and life.

With spiritual reproduction in mind, I introduce these rhythms to offer a unique yoke to help us experience God, leverage our faith for others' benefit, and reproduce a living faith in those closest to us. These rhythms are not meant to be theologically exhaustive. Instead, I intend to create something intentionally relational, missional, and most of all, transferable. I hope we reimagine the church as a more thoughtful disciple-making community of faith.

RHYTHMS CREATE MOVEMENT

In the book of Acts, the Jews started carrying out a ministry in Jesus' name that they didn't even fully understand. At least, they didn't understand what it would become. At the time, they were still thinking of it as a ministry to "their people," that somehow they had cornered the market on the divine. Although the Jews were God's chosen people, God's redemption wasn't limited to them alone—and eventually, this movement led to something different from what the Jews expected . . . yet precisely what God intended. Ministry is about creating a movement. It's about planning the first steps, igniting the kindling, and seeing where it sparks and what lights into flame.

People create movements, not programs. Movements are harder to predict than programs, and creating them requires greater faith. But they also present the most significant opportunity for God's plan to emerge.

The rhythms in this book are intended to create movement, both within us and within our communities. They present three opportunities:

1. *They enable us to experience the heart of God.* If the 2020 COVID-19 quarantine taught us anything, it's that we need new ways to experience God when the band is not present to play live, the pastor is not there to teach, and the church is not gathered to hug, laugh, and pray together. Sure, we can connect with God individually through recorded preaching or a podcast, but it's not the same as when we're fully present with other believers. These rhythms provide ways to embody and express God's heart.

2. *They leverage our faith for the benefit of others.* More than personal salvation from eternal damnation, faith should bring about "the peace and prosperity of the city [in which you live]. . . . Because if it prospers, you too will prosper" (Jeremiah 29:7). Faith needs outward expressions, and those expressions won't always make it seem like there's a return on our investment of time, money, and energy. Yet as we sow the seeds, God causes faith to germinate in people's hearts and lives (1 Corinthians 3:6-9).

3. *They help us share with those closest to us.* From the beginning of Christianity, faith was meant to be reproduced (Luke 6:40; 10:1-24; 2 Timothy 2:2). The goal was not simply to bring others to Christ but also to disciple them. Spiritual reproduction is absent in programmatic, content-rich Christian education, and we can help fill in this gap. These rhythms can aid our attempt to impart a practical, dynamic, and articulate faith to our children and to other people we might disciple.

So what is belief without corresponding action? In light of the rhythms developed here, I want to encourage people toward an integrated, more intentional pursuit of faith. But this field guide is more than just a resource for personal spiritual disciplines; it offers you a way to invest your life and make disciples.

HOW TO USE THIS FIELD GUIDE

While I'm technically providing you with seven rhythms, really it's just one rhythm expressed in seven ways. Small-batch disciplemaking is all about apprenticing in the way of Jesus. It's learning to instill in others the life in Christ that you have experienced to this point! I've heard too many accounts of earnest Christians who have grown up in the church and were active in youth group, mission trips, small groups, and even leadership say, if they were asked to disciple someone, "I wouldn't know what to say or where to start!" This field guide is offered as a manual to help you experience God, practice faith, and share with others in word and deed. Too often, discipleship gets reduced to an exchange of information over coffee or in a classroom. This resource is intended to be a companion to people with a ministry outlet who serve together.

> If you've been drawn to someone younger or newer in their faith and wanted to invest, this resource can help you equip them.

> If you've ever been asked to mentor another person, this field guide will offer structure as you serve together.

> If you're in an accountability group, part of a ministry, or on a leadership team, this framework is a way to think about forming Christ in you while you serve.

> If you're a young couple entrusted with the spiritual leadership of children, this field guide can help you articulate and reproduce a living faith.

More than anything, it's for people of faith—on a journey with God—to have a resource to help them make disciples and accelerate the Kingdom of heaven on earth. My encouragement is to:

> *Read this with another person*, presumably someone further along in their journey with Christ or someone you'd like to see grow and develop. Life change doesn't happen in a bubble. We need others to speak into our lives as much as we need to invest in others. Find a person or group to "think out loud" with.

Pair this reading with a ministry context. Since the focus is on putting into practice what we believe is true about God, identify a specific "laboratory" to experiment and express these rhythms together in. For instance, maybe you're part of an elder team, children's ministry, or other ministry team whose members would benefit from trying these rhythms with you, or perhaps you're in a small group doing life together with intentionality. Or you might be a parent with friends also looking to instill a more integrated faith in their kids.

Read this with an eye to whom you might mentor using this resource. In other words, look to become a disciplemaking Christian.

Take your time going through each rhythm. Take two to three weeks to discuss, study, and apply each chapter in this book. While it's tempting to race through a chapter each week, I would encourage you not to reduce this to a seven-week book study. Instead, give the content time to work on you. Remember, disciplemaking is a relational, intentional process.

Each chapter outlining a rhythm includes an interactive section called "Finding Your Rhythm." This is a chance to personalize your experience, apply the rhythms, and help you find your voice to share with others. Take the time to think over the content, write down your responses, and talk it through.

Your work in these interactive sections will make a big difference in how this resource will impact you. If you blow past them, you will miss out on the more profound work involved in personal interaction or discussion. Keep in mind that these sections will become your own "lesson plans" to go through this field guide with someone else!

There are also discussion questions for each chapter. These questions are meant to be discussed with others, such as an apprentice, accountability partner, leadership team, small group, or your children. Tweak them to fit your context, and use them to help mobilize others.

TWO CRITICAL QUESTIONS TO BEGIN THIS JOURNEY

1. Who are you going through this developmental process with? Again, it's best not to read this field guide independently but instead to read it in community. This could be as a mentor, an apprentice, a team, or with a small group of peers.

2. What is your primary "laboratory" where you can experiment with and animate these rhythms? Define your lab as a ministry context where you're actively serving alongside one another.

DISCUSSION QUESTIONS

1. How was faith expressed in your home growing up?

2. Who taught you to know Christ in a personal way? How did they show you this?

3. What are your earliest memories of thinking *That must be what God is like?*

4. Are there ways that your faith has gone further than or outgrown the faith of your parents?

1

THE RHYTHM
OF APPRENTICING
Rediscovering Christianity's Mission and Trade

[Jesus said,] "The student is not above the teacher,
but everyone who is fully trained will be like their teacher."
LUKE 6:40

A FRIEND ONCE TOLD ME a funny story about a time she attended a baby shower. As she mingled with the other women, a hungry three-year-old boy was looking for his mother so she could breastfeed him. He was the baby of the family—the last of four kids—and he was struggling to be weaned. As he struggled to get the attention of his mother, the situation came to a boiling point. In the middle of this room filled with women, the frustrated toddler desperately looked around and cried out loudly, "Would someone here just feed me?"

COMING OF AGE
Growing up is hard to do at every stage. It's especially true when we're used to having things done for us. Everyone experiences

growing pains as they learn to become independent (and for some it takes a little longer than others), but eventually we learn how to do things for ourselves.

We understand what it means to grow up physically, but not as many people truly understand what it means to grow up spiritually. For those of us who go to church, we're immersed in a culture of consumption. Churches are built like a department store of religious goods and services where there's something for everyone. We go to church to be fed, and while that's not a bad thing, it's not the end goal. At some point, if our faith is going to be meaningful or impactful, we need to grow up spiritually. Growing up spiritually means that eventually, we will not only develop an ability to feed ourselves but also consider how we might nourish others.

The Hebrew model of learning was about *who* you followed. The Greek model was more about *what* you were studying. So the Hebrew model was more like a laboratory and shared experience, while the Greek model was more of a lecture focused on content. So much of modern-day discipleship elicits thoughts of Sunday school, Christian education, and/or going through a book with another person. But the rhythm of apprenticing suggests on-the-job training under the supervision of a journeyman. It's about having instruction, getting dirty, being led, and learning ministry. We can only grow so far on our own, looking from afar, applying what we know before we hit a wall . . . or a desert . . . or a storm. The potential for growth is more significant than ever, but we simply can't experience it without a guide or an apprenticing leader.

In Jesus' day, the Torah (the first five books of the Hebrew

Bible) was considered a way of life. Many discussions centered around the most critical mitzvot (good deeds). The better the rabbi, the fewer the words and letters needed to summarize the commands. Daily discussions in Temple courts centered around these interpretations and which were most important. Debates could be won with a rabbi's ability to summarize the Book of the Law. When asked about the greatest mitzvot, Jesus said, "'Love the Lord your God with all your heart and with all your soul and with all your mind.' This is the first and greatest commandment. And the second is like it: 'Love your neighbor as yourself.' All the Law and the Prophets hang on these two commandments" (Matthew 22:37-40).[1] Jesus summarizes 613 commands with: *Love God* and *Love others as much as yourself.* This was a mic drop moment! No one else had ever cut through the legalism, points of emphasis, and sheer volume with this essential expediency!

Jesus says, "Come, follow," which is an invitation and an example. We ought to "yoke" our lives not only with someone who is further along than we are but also with someone who is earlier in their faith journey. In an agricultural society, Jesus' hearers would've understood the image of being yoked to God's commands. While God's commands might appear restrictive, they're to be understood as being for our good. And following requires more than simple acknowledgment; it requires practice. The metaphor doesn't end there, though. For their oxen to be effective in plowing, farmers yoke a young, energetic ox with an older ox. They find younger oxen tend to push hard at the beginning of the day, using up all their energy with nothing left for the second half. However, when yoked with an experienced ox, a younger ox learns a needed rhythm so that he can last the whole day and keep an even, sustained pace. What a needed image for fruitful and sustaining faith!

While in Jesus' day many rabbis had made their interpretation and points of emphasis strict and legalistic, Jesus, a master rabbi Himself, came with a different invitation: "My yoke is easy [i.e., useful] and my burden [or load] is light" (Matthew 11:30). Perhaps Jesus was comparing the harsh rule of Roman oppression with the life-giving obedience to God's commands. Jesus wants to show what life in the Kingdom of God on earth looks like.

The good news is that most Christians already have what it takes to disciple or apprentice someone else, even if they don't feel ready to. Just like some parts of parenting are impossible to prepare for, it's impossible to feel ready for challenges associated with leading people at any age, with any background, and in any context. Instead, we must take the leap and honor God's call. That's where the rhythm of apprenticing comes in.

WHAT IS APPRENTICING?

Have you ever had a coach, teacher, youth worker, or family member see something in you and help bring it out? Few places in our society exist where people see and help develop personal potential. Yet this is the most significant way we can steward our influence! Apprenticeship is more than encouragement or advice giving—it is an arrangement in which someone learns an art, trade, or job under another person skilled in that area.

The best way to illustrate this is from my experience as a laborer. My dad was a journeyman-carpenter-turned-dentist. He was a man who was good at working with his hands and didn't like the idea of paying someone to do a job that he could likely figure out on his own. And he wanted to instill that same ethic in me. When I returned from college in the summers, I worked in construction to learn the carpentry trade. While I only think of myself as a "rough carpenter" and not a craftsman, I still gained invaluable experience. One summer, I started work on a new build just as the foundation had been poured. In the following three months, I saw a house go from 20 percent to 80 percent completion. Each day was a chance to shadow skilled laborers handling various aspects of the building process. From handling different tools to being tasked with completing jobs, I got on-the-job training under the direction of seasoned tradespeople. Now I find myself doing similar projects with my kids, buying them tools, and watching them work—to pass this legacy on and see it grow in them, too.

Apprenticeship is a tradesperson's language: Learning a trade requires an on-the-job, hands-on relationship with someone with expertise in that trade. I believe we need the same type of relationships in Christian contexts in order to help believers mature in their faith. In a spiritual sense, apprenticeship is learning to animate the life of Christ in proximity to others. It is not about cloning or replicating others to look, talk, act, and even believe identically. Instead, apprenticing means identifying someone further along than you as well as finding newer or younger followers you can come alongside. It's finding a relational rhythm of stewarding one's influence, experience, knowledge, and understanding of Christ in the world.

A quick note about terms. I use the words *apprenticing* and *disciplemaking* interchangeably. While there might be some nuance, they get at the same idea. Both terms are verbs that are active, dynamic, progressing, and unfolding, like life and relationships. In the ancient world, this was what it meant to be a disciple. More than just a student of your rabbi's faith life, you were to learn about your rabbi's whole life. The term *mentoring* conveys a similar idea. No matter which term you prefer to use, the kind of developmental relationship I'm talking about here is experiencing and expressing the Christian life incarnationally, missionally, and with the intent of spiritual reproduction.

Sometimes this happens in organic and informal ways where gifts are applied, weaknesses are observed, and impressions are made. Hebrews 13:7 says, "Remember your leaders, who spoke the word of God to you. Consider the outcome of their way of life and imitate their faith." To be sure, we all need (and need to become) examples to follow. Stewarding one's faith with words and practice is a critical response to a Christian witness. But apprenticeship goes even further.

In the context of small-batch disciplemaking, one of the most significant opportunities we have is to speak to someone's potential. The discipler's role is to see the potential in another person—seeing who they can become in Christ based on their gifts, strengths, personality, desires, and experience—and to help identify a trajectory for them in ministry and leadership.

When I meet a younger believer, I often like to begin statements with "I see in you . . ." because people need help seeing what they can't see for themselves. Maybe they lack confidence or have never been given a chance. Perhaps no one's ever expressed belief in them. God wants to unleash their potential for helping, serving, and leading. As a mentor, you get to be part of that commissioning. When you know someone well enough to evaluate their abilities and help them see who they can become, you provide an alternative to self-loathing, shame, and struggling self-esteem. The best teachers and coaches do this, but finding someone to draw a trajectory of who we can become is rare. This is not prosperity coaching but a developmental journey you and your apprentice take together.

In 2 Timothy 2:2, Paul implores Timothy not just to teach but to train. He writes, "The things you have heard me say in the presence of many witnesses entrust to reliable people who will also be qualified to teach others." Instead of merely transferring knowledge to people, we are instructed to teach others how to lead others. This is spiritual reproduction that is central to the great commission. It's good to go through foundational content together (i.e., Scripture, outlines, or books), but this is not just to reinforce fundamental Christian beliefs or teach anything new. Jesus invited disciples to "come, follow Me," and He used His influence with them, His understanding of God's mission, and everyday circumstances to train them. See if this model feels familiar from what you've read in the Gospels:

I do it, and *you watch*. I do it, and *you help*.
You do it, and *I watch*. You do it, and *someone else watches*.

We can do a lot entirely on our own to change, grow, and develop. Yet another person who knows us well and can speak to our potential can be invaluable in this process. That person can remind us of who we are and can know when something's amiss. Life-changing relationships—the kind Jesus hosted with His closest followers—are created through invitation and challenge. He invited them to "come, follow Me" and challenged them to "go into all the world, teaching them everything I have taught you" (Matthew 28:19, PAR). In the garden of Gethsemane, He asked them to pray and then challenged them to stay awake (Matthew 26:36-46). He invited them to proclaim the Kingdom of God and challenged them not to take any additional provisions with them (Matthew 10:1-15). In every close relationship that Jesus had, He included an invitation to learn something and a sincere challenge to grow in its application. Invitation and challenge were how He would build His church through disciples.

Most Western churches hold to a content-heavy, event-based educational philosophy, which encourages us to follow "at the feet of" educated clergy and religious personalities rather than live "in the shadow of" our disciplers. This has cost Christianity essential apprenticeship, formation, and mission! What if, instead, we think of Christian apprenticeship as equal parts education (content), equipping (training), and immersion (experience)?

THE RHYTHM OF APPRENTICING: JESUS' "IDEA"

In Robert Coleman's influential book *The Master Plan of Discipleship*, he reveals how Jesus' three-year public ministry had a laser-like focus: *training the few to reach the many*.[2] Jesus wasn't set on launching a service and attracting a crowd. While He did engage the masses, these times with the crowds were illustrative and meant to equip the disciples for His eventual absence.

You remember the story of Jesus feeding the five thousand, right? We assume the story's focus is the five thousand people who needed something to eat. But in reality, most of these people were probably unaware that a miracle was occurring. The masses were gathered in a field without a public address system. They had no cameras or stadium monitors. They didn't know how many fish Jesus started with; they were just happy to get a free meal. But the Twelve acted as ushers in a sea of people. They were likely the only ones who realized that the baskets weren't running out of fish and chips! Jesus was focused on spiritually instilling in them a kind of living faith. Jesus created "laboratory" environments where He'd give the disciples a chance to experiment with faith, learning, power, and authority.

The idea of being a spiritual leader is daunting for most, but it's not impossible. As I began my apprenticing journey with my college pastor, Tim introduced me to Jesus' "IDEA." Perhaps the most significant difference between the early church and the church today is that we've gotten away from Jesus' strategy of training the few to train many. Most development, including on-the-job training, is focused on training to produce, perform, or manage. Rarely, if ever, is attention directed at training people to train others. We miss out on spiritual reproduction and, ultimately, multiplication. Yet spiritual reproduction on any scale creates a significant personal impact and an enduring legacy. So how can we step into the role of an effective mentor?

We can study how the Master Disciplemaker mentored others. Jesus' intentional approach to crafting disciples and growing faith has four main components:

1. Instruction,
2. Demonstration,
3. Experience, and
4. Assessment.

Let's look at each component of Jesus' "IDEA" approach in turn.

Instruction

Teaching an apprentice biblical truth and how to lead in ministry is good, but teaching them how to ask good questions is even better. As I entered a discipling relationship with Tim, Christianity became more than a cultural or family expression. It became a living faith. That is, it became something to nurture, practice, trust, share, and leverage for good. I was invited into proximity with my mentor, and I was eager to give whatever time I had to be available. I could observe Tim's marriage, family, leadership, and ministry up close. I got to ask lots of *Why?* questions. I began serving and leading with constant feedback, which meant that I had someone gently speaking to my potential growth, undeveloped strengths, and limiting blind spots.

Demonstration

Apprenticeship involves modeling what ministry looks like and what is required, personally and publicly, of a mentor. Tim demonstrated a concept that still pays dividends. He said, "David, it's not too difficult for someone to lead others who are younger. And most people can offer some guidance and leadership among peers. But to be effective in leadership, you need to learn to find your voice and encourage people who might be your parents' age." And then he went on to demonstrate this. Though he was only in his thirties, Tim led the Global Missions Committee, which was comprised of people in their fifties, sixties, and seventies, ranging from business leaders to retired grandparents. Tim guided discussions, fielded requests, and managed action items while giving this diverse team strategic ownership of the vision for reaching unreached people groups.

Experience

After teaching and modeling, it is good to give opportunities for responsibility as you observe that the mentee is ready. Let the person being discipled take the lead in teaching a class, facilitating a group discussion, hosting an event, organizing a ministry initiative, or guiding a team. In my willingness to "come and follow" with Tim's guidance, I was expected to be helpful in ministry but also challenged to grow in leadership. I joined our global missions team to help coordinate international trips. I also led a weekly ministry team and followed up with every visitor who indicated they wanted to learn more about the Christian faith. I didn't feel qualified, but Tim supported me. I had instruction and demonstration and was trusted with vital ministry to gain needed experience. And there were regular times for feedback, coaching, and suggestions. This was Jesus' strategy of training the few to reach the many!

Please note: The experience you're gaining is valuable whether the path you're on is toward vocational ministry or not. The world is desperate for ministers beyond the church walls. The point is to gain experience in practicing a living faith that—in a curated way that's unique to you and your voice—could be used to invest in someone else. This is where these rhythms become most helpful. Whether you're a teaching assistant at an elementary school, a Little League coach, a tradesman, a retiree, or working alongside a professional colleague who's sorting through what it means to have a living faith, you're helping advance God's Kingdom. These rhythms become a basis for a relational, incarnational, and missional life together.

Assessment

I vividly remember being invited to meet Tim in his office and asked to close the door behind me. He said, "David, this is what I heard. This is what I said in your defense. Now, tell me if you made a liar out of me." To be honest, I don't even remember the misunderstanding (there were many). What I remember was his support. He knew my character and my immaturity. I was afforded the benefit of the doubt *and* lots of mentoring. Accountability and correction were easier to accept because I understood that Tim had my best interests in mind. He saw potential and would often share what he could see in me.

If we think of apprenticing within this framework, any Christian can instill a spiritual legacy in another by offering a little instruction, modeling Jesus' life, giving experiences, and offering feedback.

Create a feedback loop. Evaluate ministry and relationships together. Create a culture of telling on yourselves. What was good, and what could've been better? Were there missed opportunities? This is a chance to reveal potential blind spots in how an apprentice comes across or sounds.

APPRENTICING MOVES AT THE SPEED OF A RELATIONSHIP

The four pieces of the IDEA framework are simple enough, but they may take time. Apprenticing is a slow, painstaking process. It moves at the speed of a relationship, not in chapters, semesters, seasons, or deadlines.

I've found a helpful illustration of this kind of apprenticing faith in a perhaps surprising place: twelve-step recovery groups. The genius of a twelve-step recovery program is that part of working out your sobriety means finding someone else to sponsor you.

If you've ever been part of a recovery meeting, you know there's a level of honesty required by the group. Alcoholics Anonymous makes room for everyone—poor, wealthy, educated, tradesman, single, married, young, old, liberal, conservative—as long as you're willing to be honest about your struggle and to take the next step. Addictions have a way of leveling the playing field and cutting away all pretense. Yet there's not only fiercely guarded safety in sharing; you also won't have to take the next step alone. When a person enters a twelve-step recovery plan, step 12 encourages you to "sponsor" someone beginning at step 1. Step 1 is when someone is finally able to say they have a problem and are powerless to help themselves. Even after you complete all twelve steps, you still battle temptation. You still feel like you're vulnerable and have room to grow. You know you need a community, *and* you need to give yourself to someone taking their first steps—or revisiting those first steps—toward sobriety.

If every Christian approached faith this way, it would transform our faith experience and revolutionize the church!

If salvation is to a Christian as sobriety is to an alcoholic, we need to have a vision to be similarly invested in one another's spiritual growth, for their sake as much as for our own. We all come to Christ the same way, willing to admit that we have a problem and are living at the center of our own stories in a broken world. And the good news isn't merely God offering us forgiveness for being self-absorbed and imperfect. God seeks to restore and redeem a broken world, and we get to be part of this restoration! And did you catch this? We participate in Kingdom work by *giving our lives away*! And perhaps the most transformational part of this process is when we find ways to apprentice or disciple another.

THE FAITH OF AN APPRENTICE

When the apostle Paul wrote to his protégé Timothy, he reminded him of their work together in previous travels. Together, they had served, taught, developed leaders, and planted churches. Having sent out Timothy on his own, Paul challenged him not just to be a great leader for the Kingdom of God but also to be a mentor to other believers. Paul wrote, "The things which you have heard from me in the presence of many witnesses, entrust these to faithful people who will be able to teach others also" (2 Timothy 2:2, NASB).

So what do you look for in a potential apprentice? It might be helpful to use the acronym FAITH to begin to either select or become an apprentice.

Faithful. Do they demonstrate a commitment to Christ? Are they already helpful in an area of ministry and service?

Available. Can they put in the time needed to meet and do ministry together?

Initiative. Are they self-motivated and hungry to learn and grow?

Teachable. Are they humble or defensive? Are they willing to change, try new things, and be accountable? Are they ready to be transparent and self-aware? Do they struggle with different authority figures in their life?

Healthy and Helpful. Is this person in a place to both give and receive challenges and invitations? Are they ready for a developmental relationship or possibly better suited for an accountability group or even a counseling relationship? One question worth asking is *Who are the healthiest people—spiritually and emotionally—you're closest to?*

APPRENTICING IN FOCUS

When you're looking for a model of early apprenticeship, the relationship between Paul and Barnabas in Acts is particularly instructive. Early in his faith walk, Paul was a man in need of a mentor. He had to live down a reputation of being overzealous and aggressive. I imagine he battled regret, shame, and even fear. He couldn't undo his past transgressions. Yet he had the basic tools: passion, hunger, knowledge, and a personal encounter with the risen Christ. That was enough for Barnabas to begin coaching him.

We don't know a whole lot about Barnabas. But the little we do know makes a strong statement about his commitment to investing in Paul as a young leader. Barnabas had some financial means, and in what we might imagine to be an idyllic early-church setting after Pentecost, he did his part to ensure "no needy persons [were] among them" (Acts 4:34).[3]

> From time to time those who owned land or houses
> sold them, brought the money from the sales and put
> it at the apostles' feet, and it was distributed to anyone
> who had need.
>
> Joseph, a Levite from Cyprus, whom the apostles
> called Barnabas (which means "son of encouragement"),
> sold a field he owned and brought the money and put it
> at the apostles' feet.
>
> ACTS 4:34-37

It says something about him that he had the means to own a piece of land. And it says a lot more that he'd sell it on behalf of the community's needs.

It doesn't seem like Barnabas needed a job description or to be asked to help. We know he was part of the early-church community and maybe even hosted a church in his home. But the next time we see Barnabas mentioned is in Acts 9: He appeared after the conversion of Paul when no one else wanted to go near him!

When [Paul] came to Jerusalem, he tried to join the
disciples, but they were all afraid of him, not believing
that he really was a disciple. But Barnabas took him
and brought him to the apostles. He told them how
Saul on his journey had seen the Lord and that the
Lord had spoken to him, and how in Damascus he
had preached fearlessly in the name of Jesus. So Saul
stayed with them and moved about freely in Jerusalem,
speaking boldly in the name of the Lord. He talked
and debated with the Hellenistic Jews, but they tried to
kill him. When the believers learned of this, they took
him down to Caesarea and sent him off to Tarsus.

ACTS 9:26-30

I suspect Barnabas sought Saul out when he first arrived, to
know him firsthand. Barnabas saw something in Saul that few
others did, something in him beyond his regretted past. He gave
Saul counsel and maybe tried to soften his edges. Saul needed
a bridge builder, which he found in Barnabas, who may have
been putting his own relationship with the apostles on the line
by embracing Saul. In Acts 9:27, we read "Barnabas took him
and brought him to the apostles." The Greek word translated
as *took* (*epilambanomai*) implies that he led Saul by the hand
before the apostles to affirm his belief in Paul, his conversion,
and his new life in Christ.

Later, Barnabas went to Tarsus to find Paul and began col-
laborating with him, developing him, believing in him, and
traveling with him as his sponsor. Paul then invited Barnabas

on a second missionary trip, but they had an argument over whether to take a young apprentice named John Mark with them. On the first journey, Mark had deserted them. Ironically, Paul was done with him, but Barnabas wanted to take him on the second journey to give him a second chance. As a result, Barnabas and Mark parted ways with Paul.

> Barnabas wanted to take John, also called Mark, with them, but Paul did not think it wise to take him, because he had deserted them in Pamphylia and had not continued with them in the work. They had such a sharp disagreement that they parted company. Barnabas took Mark and sailed for Cyprus, but Paul chose Silas and left.
>
> ACTS 15:37-40

How could Barnabas, the mentor, leave Paul at this point? Wasn't this a coaching moment to help Paul with a personality clash or a gentle reminder of where he started? Perhaps the lesson to be learned from Barnabas's decision to take Mark with him to Cyprus is that no one peaks in their performance until another person believes in them. In a beautiful picture of reconciliation, the apostle Paul later came full circle in his opinion of Mark, writing, "Only Luke is with me. Get Mark and bring him with you, because he is helpful to me in my ministry" (2 Timothy 4:11).

Becoming an apprenticing leader is not about being an expert. It's simply about being willing to share what you do know. What's most helpful and will impact lives is when we learn to put words to the difference Christ makes in our daily struggles and mundane situations. Consider that Barnabas didn't need a position, a title, or recognition to make a difference. He wasn't recruited but instead willingly invested his life, staked his reputation, and gave his time to take Paul under his wing. If we look at this as a case study for investing our lives, we can make a few simple but critical observations.

1. *Barnabas spoke to and about Paul's potential.* We aren't privy to their one-on-one conversations, but one thing is clear: Barnabas staked his own reputation when he brought Paul to the apostles to speak on Paul's behalf. His message? This guy has changed; he can grow and be part of leading this Kingdom of God movement!

2. *They shared ministry.* As I've said before, discipleship requires a "laboratory," not just a lecture or a book. The way to reveal a living faith is by living your faith out in serving and doing what you believe in. Just like the way you parent by practice and not by proxy, doing ministry together provides an opportunity to challenge assumptions, model strategies, and develop skills. Most people want to grow, but many miss out on a critical element of the process. Some are given responsibility but without proper instruction. Others gain experience yet receive little feedback. Mentoring means identifying opportunities to help equip and inspire. Consider this as you prepare to seek to multiply the life of Christ in another: Your ability to "pass the baton" and see others run will create a lasting impact.

3. *We can imagine that Barnabas held Paul accountable.* It's fascinating to me that for as much impact as Barnabas had in advocating for the apostle Paul, we don't hear about him again. But we see how he shaped Paul's church-planting ministry by raising leaders. In Paul's letter to Philemon, he advocated for the runaway-slave-turned-brother-in-Christ Onesimus. I wonder if it's Barnabas's coaching we hear in the background as Paul penned this letter from jail. This kind of growth and development happens only by investing, caring accountability.

Noted storyteller Jonah Sachs said, "The mentor's role is to make change irresistible but not mandatory."[4] It's not as much about enforcing rules as about reminding them of who they are, what they're capable of, and what you believe is possible. In a trusting relationship, we need people to hold up a mirror to our lives and show us what it looks like. For example, "When you say that . . . it sounds like this . . ." Or "I'm not sure you realize it, but when you do this . . . it can come across like . . ." It's a gentle but effective method to suggest a better way.

4. *Barnabas was open to the prompting of the Holy Spirit.* Whether it was a prompt to divest himself of property on behalf of the faith community or the poor, discerning an authentic change in Paul when every other believer feared him, or being willing to let Paul move on without him because of feeling led to give John Mark a second chance, Barnabas had a sensitivity and an obedience to the Spirit of God. Jesus often painted

a picture of the disciples doing what he did and talked of them discipling others. He sent them off in pairs so that they could lean on each other. He got them used to working together rather than alone. He expected their faith would be transferable—the knowledge, the conviction, and the concern for others' spiritual growth.

Again, the mission of the church is to make disciples, not converts, volunteers, attendees, or members. Discipleship might involve all those things. But it must go much deeper. For faith to take root, we have to leave room for discomfort as much as we embrace comfort. We need to allow for sacrifice as much as we want to allow for provision. This is how faith grows. It's how it becomes believable. It's how it transforms hearts. The good news is that we can all identify with the struggles, hurdles, valleys, and deserts already. And it's when we look back that we might even begin to see the hand of God in the sequence of our lives.

DISCUSSION QUESTIONS

1. Describe a skill or trade you learned over time. Who guided you and then critiqued your development? Can you identify any "breakthrough" moments in your process? If you were primarily self-taught, what did you miss by not having someone more skilled or further along mentoring you?

2. How do you think being a disciple differs from being a convert or believer?

3. What do you think made Jesus' disciples good candidates to build the future of the church on?

4. What lessons did they learn? What obstacles did they overcome or endure?

5. Has anyone ever referred to you as a mentor? In what way? What do you think it meant to them?

6. Can you point to someone you've intentionally invested in? What were the goals and outcomes of this investment?

7. What metaphor comes to mind when you think of being and becoming an apprentice? Is there a film, story, analogy, or Scripture passage that would help you instill this rhythm in your life?

Finding Your Rhythm

Your Apprenticing Timeline:
Finding God in the Sequence of Your Life

IDENTIFYING GOD in the larger story of your life will help you share with others your story of life in Christ. Only when we step back and piece together meaningful events, experiences, and relationships can we understand and articulate our stories better. First, look at how your life has unfolded to this point. Then consider how God was present and at work in the unfolding. It works better to avoid doing this in one sitting. Take time to think it over and revisit it a few times.

It's hard to see God's hand in a particular event, especially in the present. It isn't until we look back later that we gain insight as to how God was at work. Maybe it helps to think of the series of events like footprints in the sand. If we can begin to find God's activity in the sequence, we can understand how God might guide, equip, and call us to serve. As you start to think through critical moments in your spiritual life, consider the following questions.

1. How can you see God in the progression of your life? In other words, are there doors that are closed?
2. Which doors have opened in the last two to three years (jobs, relationships, invitations, opportunities)?

The timeline below asks questions like *Where have you been?* and *What events, people, decisions, and opportunities have shaped your life in Christ?* Remember, closed doors are part of God's confirmation. While they might be disappointing, they provide the guidance we seek from God.

MAPPING YOUR TIMELINE

Think through the following three categories, and map your responses on the timeline on pages 40-41.

1. *Peaks and valleys.* What major events and circumstances have marked your life's journey to this point? They can be positive or negative. On your timeline, list above and below the line significant decisions, people, accomplishments, and events that have shaped you into who you are today. (Remember: This is hard to do in one sitting. It's helpful to come back to it as you think through the impact of formative times.)

2. *Speed bumps, detours, and the scenic route.* What were some speed bumps along the way? Even with goals in mind, you can't avoid adversity and setbacks. You absorbed and overcame these lows along the way. While you may never want to go through them again, they likely proved to be formative. Consider the following questions:

   • What struggles in the past helped shape your faith and resolve today?
   • Did you get helpful, surprising, or unsettling feedback?
   • What doors closed? Where did you hear the clearest nos?
   • Are there any difficult circumstances that, in looking back, you realize God has used to strengthen your faith or character?

3. *Themes and lessons.* What themes seem to recur in your conversations, relationships, or Scripture reading? Are there subjects you return to regularly in prayer or reading? (A few examples include community, obedience, calling, surrender, lordship, generosity, spiritual gift identification, personal intimacy with God, concern for the vulnerable and marginalized, and service during different seasons of growth.)

   • Can you think of significant life events or key decisions that shaped your life in Christ?
   • Was there a relationship that taught, encouraged, or challenged you to address a blind spot that was inhibiting your growth?

EARLY LIFE

PRESENT

APPLYING WHAT YOU'VE LEARNED

Memorize 2 Timothy 2:2: "The things you have heard me say in the presence of many witnesses entrust to reliable people who will also be qualified to teach others."

Begin applying this verse as you serve in ministry with and for others. Also begin thinking about, discussing with others, and asking God whom you might apprentice and minister alongside.

2

THE RHYTHM OF RENEWAL

Developing a Growing Awareness of God's Presence

*[Jesus said,] "The time has come. . . . The kingdom of God
has come near. Repent and believe the good news!"*

MARK 1:15

WHEN OUR DAUGHTER, ANNIKA, was born twenty-two
months after our son, I thought I should write a journal for
her. Journaling is not my thing, but having a daughter was new
territory. I wanted to be thoughtful in nurturing our daddy-
daughter relationship. At the same time, as a pastor and father,
I was restless about raising pastors' kids, who often unfairly
spend too many hours at church and draw the attention of
every parishioner. I wanted to instill in them a living faith,
a love for Jesus, not simply a Sunday-go-to-church faith. I had
a distinct impression, which I took as a prompt from the Lord,
that said, *You've gotten it half right.* It was one of those unique,
rare moments where I felt the Spirit saying, *Yes, be Christ to
her. But I also want to teach you about Me through her, so take*

43

note! And so, for thirteen years, I kept a handwritten journal of how God's Spirit was teaching me to grow in faith through my interactions with my daughter. While it wasn't a natural discipline for me, it became a great practice for allowing God to continually resensitize my heart.

Here's an entry from one of those "divine interruptions," recorded when Annika was fifteen months old:

> Last night, you were up a couple of different times,
> which isn't unusual as you're still breastfeeding. While I
> could hear you crying—and with me wanting to sleep—
> I asked the Lord to help me see and experience Him.
> And at that moment, it was like I heard an immediate
> response! It was as if God was speaking through your
> tears—and an untimely interruption into my rest—
> THAT'S ME!! Those are My cries to want to be with
> you at all times! It was like God was saying, "Don't just
> roll over and think you can find Me later." Instead, I
> got up to find you standing in your crib. Normally, you
> have a one-track mind, wanting Mommy and to be fed.
> But this was different. I held you, and we talked, me
> with words and gestures. I said, "I'm here. Daddy loves
> you." You put your head on my shoulder, and we held
> each other . . . until we were both comforted. It was
> 2:00 a.m., but God's presence (and lesson) was noticed.

The rhythm of renewal is about regularly and continually resensitizing our hearts so we can hear God's whisper, respond when the Spirit guides, and yield when God prompts. As mature disciplemakers, a rhythm of renewal enables us to be attentive to the Holy Spirit *so that* being attentive to what God is saying will help us speak prophetically to young believers. If our goal is to be effective small-batch disciplemakers, practicing the rhythm of renewal will help us get there.

So first, what does our rest produce? Scripture doesn't invite us to sleep, vacation, unload responsibilities, or pursue a more convenient way of living. Renewal isn't meant to restore our margins so we can live the life we want to live. Nor does it mean the struggle or tension in life goes away; rather, biblical renewal recenters and resensitizes our hearts to God's presence.

Maybe most people don't experience more growth because it's sadly normal to allow our hearts to grow calloused. We often insulate ourselves from getting too upset or feeling too vulnerable. So how can we remain responsive and grow closer to God when we guard our hearts? By practicing the rhythm of renewal, which recenters us on the one who gives life. Renewal invites us to combat a culture that feeds our ambition, consumption, and insecurities. Growth of any kind takes time because it involves both unlearning old habits *and* discovering a new way to live. The renewal process allows us to change from the inside out, by renewing our minds and resensitizing our hearts (Romans 12:2). It can be saddening, challenging, and even painful, but that doesn't mean goodness, beauty, and new life don't emerge! The goal is that we might be made new, more like the image of God, *and* participate in His redemption and restoration. Again, to do that, we need our hearts to be resensitized.

Second, how can we steward our influence while keeping in mind the Spirit's role? With an apprentice, it's important to speak to their potential about who they can become in Christ. This is one of the most critical and life-giving (yet rarely taught) aspects of the Christian's life. Without trying to be a prophet, every believer can (and should) learn to speak prophetically to younger and teachable believers. As God gives you insight and your relationship with an apprentice deepens, you will be better able to speak to their spiritual and ministry potential.

Often, small decisions make a big difference over time, just as shifting a mere two degrees will create a radically different trajectory for an entire journey. I never like to say, "God told me . . ." when speaking into someone's life. But when I have an impression—that may or may not be from God—I like to simply offer it by saying, "I had this idea . . . see if this resonates." If I've heard from God, I don't need to be persuasive to get the message across.

What's also happening in this rhythm of renewal is that we are developing a model for sensitivity. We can be busy and still be attentive to God's Holy Spirit. It takes practice, but over time we can become more, if not very, familiar with how God is speaking and guiding us. And the best way to learn this spiritual discernment isn't in a classroom or from a sermon but in the safety of a developmental relationship with someone further along.

REFRAMING THE SABBATH

"Be tired later" were the words my high school basketball coach would often say when we huddled up in the fourth quarter with a game on the line. It was a great motivational reminder to finish strong and stay mentally focused. It implied that the end was near and helped us not to let up. What works for a basketball game doesn't always translate to life, however. Now, as an adult, my days often run long, and work bleeds into the weekends. Spiritual, mental, physical, and emotional margins can get thin, but the needs, opportunities, and responsibilities don't let up. Maybe it's the blue-collar work ethic my parents instilled in me, but it's hard for me not to keep pushing, telling myself to "be tired later." Rather than a good motivation to finish strong, this saying can become a license to work without boundaries.

Sabbath has always been God's way of renewing us. But this kind of rest is not to be an end in itself. Sabbath rest doesn't mean inactivity. It's not about channel surfing or even long naps. It's not to recharge our batteries so we can focus our energy on ourselves. It's the idea that *we work from our rest, not rest from our work.* We mostly get this backward in our society, which is why so many of us typically operate with thin emotional margins and calloused hearts, and miss opportunities to experience the prompts of God's Spirit. But when we work from our rest, we connect with God's Spirit and find strength, comfort, peace, and hope. We can see what we do have rather than what we lack. The discipline of a weekly Sabbath is not unlike tithing because it requires us to ask ourselves: *Do I trust God with my resources (time or money)?* We find a rhythm of renewal in the Sabbath, which resensitizes our hearts, minds, and bodies to live within God's Spirit.

An old farmer once told me of the practice of *laying by.* It referred to the time on a farm between busy seasons. It meant resting and waiting *but not* being inactive. It was when you made improvements to the property, like digging a new well or reroofing the barn, that would have a long-term benefit. Or you did maintenance on farm equipment to prepare for the coming season.

Laying by is a helpful concept for small-batch disciple-making. Developing a rhythm of renewal means we're preparing for when—not if—the rug gets pulled out from under us. Renewal isn't a luxury but a necessity if we are to grow in Christ. Faith is often (re)ignited when something overwhelming happens—a death, a health scare, a job loss, or the birth of a child. But once we get acclimated to the situation, we lose a sense of urgency. It is easy to put off faith and community and live without a sense of mission.

More than a day of rest or relaxation, a rhythm of renewal invites a disciplined observance. In some instances, it means keeping a standing appointment for faith and community. In other cases, it can mean finding time to be quiet before God and drown out the competing voices and false narratives. The ancient observance of Sabbath was as much about trusting God with the demands and responsibilities of life as it was about worshiping God. Like an interruption to the relentless pursuit of our survival and ambition, God seeks to be at the center of our hearts. And that requires constant recalibration.

Our lives are supposed to be a harvest, but growth requires fertile soil. Renewal means tilling the soil of your heart and mind as each of us learns to yield to God's Spirit—a nudge to turn from or turn toward something or someone. Simply put, a renewed heart is a sensitive heart. And we can grow more familiar with God's voice, but only to the extent that we respond! This is the process of spiritual transformation. We might not even be aware of what the Spirit is doing. But we start with doing what we know to do, and then God increasingly begins to direct our lives.

AN ANTIDOTE FOR EXHAUSTION

If you want to avoid dehydration, drink before you're thirsty. It sounds like a simple enough rule, but it's easier said than done. Our days get busy, we forget to drink, and the progression happens subtly: We go from being parched to having a headache, which becomes fatiguing. And fatigue, unattended, quickly spirals. Before we know it, we're sick.

Ever been there, physically? What about relationally, financially, creatively, or spiritually? Dry seasons are part of every career, home, marriage, *and* personal faith. Refreshment is needed. Renewal helps us live in the power of the Resurrection. Jesus' resurrection almost two thousand years ago became a promise of new life for all people in all times and circumstances who choose to believe. Not just once and for all but continually and daily. To be renewed by the Spirit of God, we need to be willing to turn to Him.

In the Judean wilderness, the ancient songwriter David wrote some anticipatory words:

> O God, you are my God;
>   I earnestly search for you.
> My soul thirsts for you;
>   my whole body longs for you
> in this parched and weary land
>   where there is no water.
> PSALM 63:1, NLT

David understood the need for refreshment for body and soul and wouldn't wander too far and for too long without spiritual hydration. We'd do well to do the same—to drink before we're thirsty. Refreshment comes in odd ways. Vacations can leave us exhausted, while intense workdays can energize us. We can be with friends and feel disconnected while a new face makes us feel known. We can labor through seasons when it seems like our prayers never go past the ceiling. Yet we also stumble across provision from God that we didn't even know to ask for.

In his book *Midlife and the Great Unknown*, David Whyte describes how he was getting pulled in many directions working at a small company and wearing many different hats. After walking home one evening, he met with a trusted friend. He said, "Friend, speak to me about exhaustion." He expected his friend to recommend a break, a holiday, a book, or a new discipline. Instead, the friend squarely replied, "David, the antidote to exhaustion isn't resting. The antidote to exhaustion is wholeheartedness!"[1]

In other words, exhaustion is not just a matter of physical, emotional, or mental fatigue. When we get spread thin, we discover the limits of care. It's not a loss of care but a limitation of how much care we can express. We subtly and unconsciously allow our hearts to desensitize over time.

Wholeheartedness is the surrendering that must occur in a disciple's life when they realize they're operating as the center of their own lives. Wholeheartedness is not about exerting more effort—it's about trusting God to care for what you want and need. It's poise and promise more than anxiety and ambition.

It's understanding that your life is best when you're not at the center and letting God help you refocus on Him.

Wholeheartedness starts to feel impossible when we realize how deeply we care. We care greatly about our kids' success in every area of life. We also care deeply about our aging parents. We care about our economic security and maximizing the enjoyment of weekends and holidays. We care about quality friendships, self-care, and "me" time. We care about our health, debt, education, the economy, democracy, freedom, those on the margins, and injustice. We spend so much time at the limits of our care that it's exhausting. It's hard to respond to one more thing.

But if the antidote to exhaustion is wholeheartedness, then we must learn how to set boundaries. Our priorities need to inform what we say yes to and permit us to say no.

DIGGING DEEPER

John Paton was a Scottish missionary to the New Hebrides islands in the South Pacific. Pastor Harry Emerson Fosdick recounted some of Paton's story in his book *The Meaning of Prayer*: "During a dry season . . . the missionary awakened the derision of the natives by digging for water. They said water always came down from heaven, not up through the earth. But Paton revealed . . . heaven could give them water through their own land."[2]

Digging deeper has a way of revealing larger truths. When we dig deeper, we bear fruit, seeding our lives with a growing awareness of the presence of God. Some people think that God is looking for results, but Scripture tells us that He's looking for fruit. The difference is that results are what happens *around us*; fruit is what happens *inside us*. Abiding in Christ enables us to bear fruit (John 15:4), but doing this means developing an awareness of God's presence as part of daily life. And this abiding is what makes intimacy with God possible. Of course, as with any relationship, we can miss cues or grow distant. More than "arriving" at intimacy with God, we need a rhythm to court and cultivate it.

When we live at a breakneck pace in a world full of secular messaging, it's hard to make sense of what God's doing to heal, redeem, comfort, and restore. Practicing renewal is an effort to live more sustainably by managing our hearts, attention, and actions.

Intimacy with God can seem like an abstract or foreign idea, but it's not when we consider the role communication plays in nurturing a relationship. Consider prayer as a form of communication. Sometimes prayer is asking God *for* things. Sometimes prayer is asking God *about* something. When I was a kid, I always asked my parents *for* things—like rides, homework help, a sleepover, a stop at 7-Eleven, or allowance money. As I grew up, I started asking them *about* things—like what it was like to live in an occupied country, not knowing how to speak the language in a new country, or how they felt when they buried their parents. I asked about doing military service, trusting the government, learning a trade, and working graveyard shifts in the family restaurant as a teenager. Similarly, spiritual growth always invites us to deeper intimacy with our heavenly Father.

Despite being given full access to the heart of the Father through the Word, the indwelling work of the Spirit, and the great cloud of witnesses, many people end up missing out and settling for "enough" of God. Enough to be saved. Enough to believe. Enough to be better than most. But not enough to be transformed from the inside out. Fosdick makes this point about Paton's story: "Men insist on waiting for God to send them blessing in some super-normal way, when all the while he is giving them abundant supply if they would only learn to retreat into the fertile places of their own spirits where, as Jesus said, the wells of living waters seek to rise."[3] Mining for heaven on earth means attempting to dig for deeper levels of trust and obedience. It's being willing to unearth the Spirit's prompts that invite us to respond to a need, an opportunity, a stranger, a neighbor, and the church.

MANAGE WHO YOU BECOME

My uncle David is a bit of a Renaissance man—bright, resourceful, well traveled, and with various interests. He's one of the people I like to listen to as he thinks out loud. One time I asked him, "What advice would you give to an eighteen-year-old leaving home?"

Without hesitation, he said, "Manage who you become! . . . Life is like a train station, and opportunities are moving in and out. You must choose opportunities that cultivate health, faith, education, interests, character, and discipline. For instance, you don't need to worry about all As on exams. If you get a B but understand the material, it's okay! Don't overemphasize academics and miss out on other valuable opportunities to develop."

The apostle Paul offers similar advice: "Be very careful, then, how you live—not as unwise but as wise, making the most of every opportunity" (Ephesians 5:15-16). In other words, a foolish person has no plan or practice for life and faith. Without a plan, we struggle to live in light of our identity in Christ. Paul exhorts believers to be wise and make the most of every opportunity. How do we do that? With God's help. Let's look at an example from the Old Testament. In Exodus 31:2-5, we find God's people being instructed in how to worship God after their deliverance from slavery in Egypt. God is forming a covenant in the light of their new spiritual identity. God says to Moses, "See, I have chosen Bezalel son of Uri, . . . and I have filled him with the Spirit of God, with wisdom, with understanding, with knowledge and with all kinds of skills—to make artistic designs for work in gold, silver, and bronze, to cut and set stones, to work in wood, and to engage in all kinds of crafts."

Did you catch it? The Spirit of God gave Bezalel the wisdom, knowledge, and skills he needed to complete his God-given task. And the Spirit of God equips us for our God-given purposes too. The basis for wisdom in the Bible is not IQ. Wisdom is not the same as intelligence. Bezalel didn't need the ancient equivalent of an advanced degree to be an artisan. Similarly, you don't need a seminary degree to know God in a more intimate or personal way. What's needed is to be faithful with what God's Spirit has already given! God animated an ability through Bezalel, which is exactly what he seeks to do in each of us. Wisdom and gifts are never static resources. They grow and develop as we use, if not leverage, them as a missional and incarnational offering.

Before we leave this idea of faithfully using God's gifts, it's important to see how managing who we become connects with disciplemaking. Like an artist, we frame our experiences and gifts around needs and opportunities. We stretch the canvas of our relationships and look for ways to animate God's wisdom and gifts in service together. Notice that Bezalel was also given an assistant, Oholiab, who likely had his own set of skills but also potential to grow (verse 6). These two were responsible for all that related to the Tabernacle and its service, though because of the magnitude of the project, they likely had to supervise various aspects of its creation. In Exodus 35:34 we read that God gave both men "the ability to teach others." Being a disciple is more than being a good volunteer. It's more than offering one's gifts or talents in service to God. The art of disciplemaking is spiritual reproduction—that is, learning to impart a lifestyle of following Christ to others. As we develop a growing awareness of God's presence as it relates to wisdom and influence, we'll be increasingly able to speak to and guide others.

THE DIVINE AFFIRMATION

At the beginning of Jesus' public ministry, He left Galilee for the Jordan River. John the Baptist was there, drawing crowds as he invited the people of God to repent and be baptized. Luke's Gospel records that Jesus "was about thirty years old when he began his ministry" (Luke 3:23). As if Jesus were just like everyone else, He waded into the Jordan River to be baptized. John initially resisted, feeling unworthy of such a task. Yet he complied. Upon Jesus' immersion, "heaven was opened and the Holy Spirit descended on him in bodily form like a dove. And a voice came from heaven: 'You are my Son, whom I love; with you I am well pleased'" (Luke 3:21-22).

Before Jesus had healed, fed, or delivered anyone from a demon; before Jesus had taught one lesson, saved one soul, or done anything to build a résumé worthy of being the Messiah; before Jesus could make Himself more lovable or worthy of God's affection, He received this blessing: "You are my Son, whom I love; with you I am well pleased." What if every child of God could begin to see themselves in the same light of the Father's love?

The apostle Paul always described people as "saints," never sinners. He called himself the "chief" of sinners (1 Timothy 1:15, KJV) but said he wasn't who he once was (1 Timothy 1:12-13). When we're firmly grounded in Christ—as a new creation— we're free to deal with our sins because our identity and worth are not in question. And once we believe this, we need to return to it often. We return to this truth despite the shame, fear, and regret. We return to it because God's love was never based on our merit. This is ground zero for a life in Christ. This rhythm of returning invites us to be renewed again and again and again as needed!

TURNING AND RE-TURNING

The rhythm of renewal provides a needed and fresh way to reimagine the critical biblical concept of repentance. When we hear the word *repentance*, we typically think of our sins, inadequacies, and shortcomings. Yet true repentance should serve as a reminder of God's unwavering love. The Hebrew word for *repentance* (*teshuvah*) refers to a "turning."[4] So a renewed heart is a sensitive heart able to turn toward or away from something based on the Holy Spirit's guidance, to *re*turn to divine affirmation. Remember the Garden. Before sin entered the world, humanity experienced God's unfiltered, unadulterated presence. The world was as God intended. No shame. No fear. No regret, accusation, greed, or corruption. Ever since Genesis 3, God has sought to repair and restore our relationship with Himself, each other, and His creation.

At the outset of His public ministry, Jesus boldly announced that the Kingdom of heaven was a present reality, not just a future destination. In other words, we can experience, even create, heaven on earth. If we look at the events of our lives as opportunities, we might have a greater sense of God at work.

> [Jesus said,] "The time has come. . . . The kingdom of God has come near. Repent and believe the good news!"
>
> MARK 1:15

There are three key segments of this verse to unpack that show us how we can help advance the Kingdom of heaven here on earth:

1. "The time has come."
2. "The kingdom of God has come near."
3. "Repent and believe the good news!"

I like to refer to this threefold process as "the practice of turning." Let's look at each part of the practice individually.

"The time has come."

The Greek word for "time" used in Jesus' announcement is *kairos*, which, in this case, refers to a present opportunity to see the Kingdom of heaven come crashing down. Among the Greek words in the New Testament used to describe time, *chronos* is the one that typically refers to measurable time, as on a clock. *Kairos*, meanwhile, could often be described as an opportunity. Sometimes, we confuse activity with accomplishment. We live our lives as a series of events but often aren't able to make sense of them. Part of the Kingdom of God being near means watching for how God is near to us and at work in the world in the present moment. Kairos moments (or opportunities) happen in big and small ways. It's one thing to look back and find God in the pattern of events in our lives. It's another—possibly more impactful—thing to observe a present opportunity, struggle, or need and respond in real time.

Kairos moments are those times you realize there's something more going on. Much of life feels ordinary and routine. Parts of life can be accidental or due to chance. Yet we also find that a few moments of life are profound, like discovering a divine aha. When we keep an eye out for these kairos moments, we become more attuned to the person and promptings of the Holy Spirit and are therefore more available to participate in Kingdom work. It is extraordinary to think that the Holy Spirit enters the mundane of our lives to participate with us in supernatural and ordinary ways!

Kairos moments can be positive or negative. Indeed, interruptions can be good and needed. Some people think of God's presence as warm, comforting, and affirming, and it can be. But

God also grieves at circumstances He didn't intend. The world's message is that what's easy is good and what's hard is bad. But if that were true, Jesus never would have ended up on the cross. The center of God's will is *not* the path of least resistance. The more we can see and sense God in the struggle, the more we'll be grounded in lasting hope.

Kairos moments can be recognized by a decision to turn. This might feel like an initial hesitation, a "check" in the spirit, or an inexplicable prompt to do something unplanned, uncomfortable, or inconvenient. These spiritual windows of opportunity signal chances to grow as we respond to the Spirit's direction.

"The kingdom of God has come near."

Many people grew up understanding heaven as the place you go when you die. As a younger Christian, I believed that I was to struggle and endure until I died or Jesus returned. But heaven was never supposed to be a goal or a destination of the Christian life. Heaven isn't supposed to be thought of as "there and then." Heaven is not simply a place we go when we die. And eternity is not something that begins when we die; eternity has already begun. Jesus' announcement that "the kingdom of God has come near" communicates the availability of God's Kingdom here and now! Despite living in a broken creation with flawed humanity, we're invited to be cocreators of heaven on earth. It's like we live in a wheat field but weeds are also around us. And as the parable of the weeds goes (Matthew 13:24-30), Jesus was adamant the weeds *not* be uprooted for fear of also uprooting the wheat.

It's important to understand that we live in a world God

created but never intended to be this way. Do you think God planned a world full of greed and corruption, miscarriages and birth defects? Do you believe God designed the world to include cancer, addiction, depression, natural disasters, school shootings, global warming, or a predisposition to obesity? This is not the paradise God envisioned. Instead, we're living with the effects of a fallen world. And ever since sin entered the human experience, God has sought to restore, repair, and redeem creation. What's more, God desires His followers to be set apart from the rest of creation as agents of healing, hope, mercy, and justice. At the same time that much of what we experience as normal feels like "hell on earth," God invites Christians to be dual citizens who can work to bring a little heaven to earth. When we talk about heaven on earth, we're talking about restoring the world as God intended in small acts of attentiveness. When we celebrate the Resurrection, we embrace the promise of "do-overs" and the chance to begin again . . . and again. We find that attempts to bring light, encouragement, support, relief, and help are not easy, comfortable, or convenient. And these attempts are often unrecognized by others. Yet God is in the hard and the good, which means we can experience peace amid this world's trouble.

"Repent and believe the good news!"

To *repent* means to think differently or reconsider. Often, the idea of repentance reminds us of shortcomings and inadequacies. The invitation from Jesus isn't to dwell or get stuck within this framework but rather to turn from it. Repentance is a means by which we are restored to God from being separated and from seeing ourselves differently from the way God views us. Repentance is a *return* to the life that God intended for us. In some instances, *repentance* means *turning from* something. Other times, it's *turning toward* something in response to God's leading.

The gospel message, in some way—and at some point—will likely disorient us. That doesn't sound like good news, but it is. No one thought Jesus' death could result in such redeeming good news for all people in all times and circumstances, but it did! Jesus' example invites us to surrender our self-sufficiency and reorient our lives in light of the Resurrection. As we lose our death grip on our personal health, safety, and finances, we realize how fragile and interconnected all human lives are. We might even realize that we were never really in control in the first place. What we do in the valley of disorder enables us to transform as we reorient our lives in Christ. The Good News represents a wake-up call as we reorder our hearts to the pulse of a living God.

This is where kairos moments fit in, when you sense something else is going on, something beyond yourself. It might be an opportunity to learn about a social justice issue in your community, a call to help a stranger experiencing a need, or an urge to pray for a poverty-stricken nation across the world. These invitations are opportunities to participate in restoring God's Kingdom on earth, to turn and align our hearts with God's heart.

A RENEWED SENSITIVITY

The call to repent is a call to examine our hearts, reconsider our courses in life, and turn toward or away from something.

Frequently, God's Spirit speaks through a personal hesitation or, as noted above, a "check" in our spirits. We want to pay attention to these nudges and consider, *Am I being asked to turn away from sin, a certain attitude, or resentment? Am I invited to turn toward compassion, patience, forgiveness, or generosity?* The sensitivity of our hearts before God will always produce a growing awareness of God's presence. This is as personal as it gets with the God of creation! But while God's Spirit convicts and leads us, He doesn't shame or guilt-trip us into obedience. We become sensitive to a first impression or initial reaction as we examine events, circumstances, and conversations, asking ourselves, *What does Scripture say? Does something need to be confessed? Who can I ask or share with? Is there a pattern, or is this connected to other events?* Ultimately, we're trying to figure out what God is saying to us.

What is belief without action? If our belief carries no response, God is only a theory! In his epistle to the early church, James wrote that "faith without works is dead" (James 2:20, KJV). The New Testament writers announced that who we are in Christ is our identity: We are each a "new creation" (2 Corinthians 5:17), which means, in Christ we're restored, reconciled, and righteous. Our pasts only *describe who we were*, which is different from *defining who we are and who we will become*. These writers believed that if believers kept learning who they were in Christ, they would know (or at least figure out) what to do. This is where disciplemaking, while practicing a rhythm of renewal, can keep us attuned to the Spirit's guidance and able to advance the Kingdom in real time.

DISCUSSION QUESTIONS

1. When is an interruption a good thing?

2. What events in your adult life have forced you to turn or change course (e.g., divorce, job loss, a diagnosis, a promotion, a near-death experience, childbirth, marriage)?

3. How have significant life interruptions helped you see or experience God's presence?

4. When you pray, are there recurring themes (beyond asking for help, provision, and safety)?

5. How would you explain the value and need for repentance to a new believer or a non-Christian? Is there a metaphor or analogy you might use to paint a picture of this rhythm of renewal?

Finding Your Rhythm

Developing an Awareness of God's Presence

IT'S ONE THING to be interrupted by the phone, our kids, a power outage, a slow driver, a Girl Scout selling cookies, a person experiencing homelessness, or a flat tire. It's another thing to be interrupted by God. But what if God were part of our everyday and regular interruptions? Would we recognize it?

Jesus said in Mark 1:15, "The time has come. . . . The kingdom of God has come near. Repent and believe the good news!" Kairos moments are opportunities to experience the Kingdom of heaven here and now. Think about that—God's perspective amid ordinary human life and struggles! The way we gain God's perspective is by turning.

INVITATIONS TO TURN

Most of us experience prompts where we feel led by God to help or respond somehow. Consider the following questions.

1. Over the past month or so, has there been a time when you've thought God was trying to get your attention?

2. What do you think God might be inviting you to do? Is there something you're supposed to turn from or toward?

3. How might you explain hearing God or sensing His presence to a seven-year-old or a skeptical friend?

PRAYER OF EXAMEN TO SENSITIZE OUR HEARTS

The Prayer of Examen is a spiritual practice of reviewing our hearts in light of God's will, and it involves asking the Spirit of God to affirm, convict, comfort, or reveal things about us. It is often prayed in the evening, as a reflection on the day's experiences and one's spiritual posture toward them. If you've never done this practice before, here are some questions and activities for you to consider.

Psalm 51:10-12 says,

> Create in me a pure heart, O God,
>   and renew a steadfast spirit within me.
> Do not cast me from your presence
>   or take your Holy Spirit from me.
> Restore to me the joy of your salvation
>   and grant me a willing spirit, to sustain me.

4. What do you think the writer means when he prays, "Renew a steadfast spirit within me"?

5. When you're in a funk (discouraged, anxious, or uncertain), are you more likely to just wait for it to pass or to do something to change your circumstances?

6. How might you become more sensitive to God's Spirit?

This week, start a "kairos journal" while you apply the rhythm of renewal. Record instances where you felt God speak or felt that something more was going on. It could be positive or negative events, and God might have spoken in either small or dramatic ways. You might write daily or weekly. The point is to be attentive. Examine and respond to experiences where you think something is meant to be learned, confessed, celebrated, or shared. As you learn to become aware of God's presence and the Holy Spirit's role in sensitizing your heart, take the time to write down moments when you sensed God was at work. The critical question to ask yourself when you sense God is: *Is there something I'm supposed to turn from and/or turn to?*

Memorize Psalm 139:23-24:

> Search me, God, and know my heart;
>   test me and know my anxious thoughts.
> See if there is any offensive way in me,
>   and lead me in the way everlasting.

Begin praying this verse in still and quiet moments. Praying this verse (or one like it) is a simple way to practice the Examen.

Jot down the words, attitudes, conversations, or faces that come to mind as you pray the Prayer of Examen.

3

THE RHYTHM OF HOSPITALITY

Discerning Whom God Has Prepared in Advance

Always be prepared to give an answer to everyone who asks you
to give the reason for the hope that you have [in Christ Jesus].
But do this with gentleness and respect.

I PETER 3:15

WHAT DO YOU GET when you cross Mexico, Louisiana, and Texas? An annual, entertaining mash-up event called "Cinco de Bayou, Y'all." Planned on the Sunday preceding May 5th (Cinco de Mayo), our scrappy little faith community in Austin, Texas, combines a crawfish boil with brisket BBQ and Mexican fajitas. It's jambalaya and queso with crawfish races, piñatas, face painting, a mechanical bull, inflatables, gaga ball, spikeball, and more. We begin with the premise that everyone is spiritual, but many folks need more time to be ready to take the next step into a worship service or a small group. So we set out to make faith and community accessible. We want to throw parties for the sake of others. We make room for friends, neighbors, and coworkers and include people with limited means, language and cultural barriers, and family distress. Imagine a couple hundred people, including recent immigrant families, suburbanites, empty nesters, agnostics, creatives, liberals and conservatives, singles and couples. Each bearing the image of a Creator God, we all gather to enjoy food and friendship.

In our second year of the event, a woman pulled me aside. An attorney by profession, she wasn't raised in the church. Removed from the crowd, we struck up a conversation. She said, "What you've created here is something I haven't seen anywhere. . . . You just don't find this kind of [ethnic and class] diversity." I explained that the narrative from prominent media sources is that if we're different, we can't get along—but that doesn't reflect the reality of my experiences.

I shared stories of visiting apartments of immigrant refugees: sitting on the floor, drinking tea, and eating dates and homemade hummus. I shared stories about survival and how coming to America was never "Plan A" for them. I spoke of Ali, who had been a translator for the US Special Forces in Afghanistan before he was forced to flee with his family for their safety. He'd graduated from college and owned a grocery store back home; now he bagged groceries for eleven dollars an hour as he and his family began rebuilding their lives. I told her other personal stories I'd learned from spending time with people across Austin. Then I explained why our church held this event each year, bringing together a broad swath of people from every background and culture.

The concept of a meal is used as a beautiful metaphor woven throughout the Bible. And at the end, in the Book of Revelation, we read: "Here I am! I stand at the door and knock. If anyone hears my voice and opens the door, I will come in and eat with that person, and they with me" (Revelation 3:20). The meal represents God's desire for relationship, which he has placed in our hearts. We want relationships with people who are like us and with those who seem unlike us—people whose immediate needs may differ from ours but who share the same Creator and the same fundamental needs for faith and friendship. This yearly party is our attempt to host a creative and fun meal at the park and see who might join us so that we might engage in boundary-crossing relationships across our city.

This is the rhythm of hospitality. As disciplemakers, before we can teach or baptize, we begin by making ourselves available and approachable. Sometimes that means inviting and hosting others. Other times, people will seek you out. In either case, the greatest witness you can make is by describing the difference Christ is making in you. This chapter is about helping you find the words for the hope you have. The good news is this: If Christ is at work in you, no one can argue or refute your experience in Christ.

Christians often need to be reminded what it's like to be new and uninitiated. Have you ever found yourself at a house party only to piece together that several couples went to college together or knew each other as singles? Good luck feeling like you can fit in! This happens to new people when they visit a church's small group, community group, or Sunday school group. They are hungry for community yet not sure how to fit in when everyone else seems so familiar with each other. When we practice a rhythm of hospitality, we might find ourselves opening our homes or preparing a meal. Whatever form hospitality takes, it is a tangible expression of God's care. It might be in the form of advice, prayer, a meal, lodging, companionship, or a favor given. But it starts with an invitation.

Traditionally, the church has talked about "evangelism," "sharing your faith," "witnessing," and "soul winning." Such language causes some of us to squirm, worried that we might not have the right words or that we're in no position to witness to others given the messy state of our own lives. But while someone might not feel like evangelism is one of their spiritual gifts, every Christian can learn to talk about the difference Christ has made in them. This means to "give the reason for the hope that [we] have" (1 Peter 3:15).

Instead of sharing a convincing argument, what if we discover and learn to articulate what Jesus' good news means to us personally? Small-batch disciplemaking must involve a rhythm of hospitality through which we engage in practices that make faith and community more accessible.

Experiencing the fullness of God is a two-way street. *The rhythm of hospitality is about both making room and learning to receive from another.* In either case, we seek to recognize those whom God has prepared in advance for us.

LEARNING TO RECEIVE

I once read this quote from The Little Free Pantry website: "To give is selfish, to receive is generous." For well-educated, upwardly mobile, hardworking folks, that is true. In our affluent Western world, many people are more comfortable being on the giving end of help or favors than on the receiving end. What do you think is behind our struggle to receive—or even ask for—help? Maybe it's humbling. Perhaps we don't like feeling indebted. But we forget that when we're willing to give *and receive* care, we open ourselves to tangible expressions of God's love. We're often so quick to say, "No thanks," "I'm fine," and "I'm okay" that we miss out on those whom God is drawing near to us for the potential of spiritual impact. I've found that receiving favors, kindness, and care from others reveals the presence of God and reminds me that He provides. If I never receive hospitality, I can easily be lulled into believing that I don't need Him.

Imagine—making Christ known by letting someone help, give to, or serve *you*! It feels counterintuitive, but this is a significant way God wants to draw people closer to Him and to each other. The way we grow relationships is by giving of ourselves. So when we resist another, we might actually be stifling the work of the Spirit.

If we want to experience God's presence, we need to allow for God's leading. When it comes to using our faith for good, maybe the best thing we can do is let someone new, someone unexpected, care for us in unexpected ways. When we do, two things happen: God provides for us and He draws people together. Think about it. We feel most alive when we can contribute. We feel most connected when we can help, give, or serve. So a person who refuses to let anyone help might turn away the opportunity to receive from God through others. Jesus said, "It is easier for a camel to go through the eye of a needle than for someone who is rich to enter the kingdom of God" (Matthew 19:24). He's not saying that God frowns on wealth. He's reminding us that abundance has a way of making us think we're self-sufficient.

Our church visited immigrants from the Middle East, Southeast Asia, and Africa, and we wanted to become part of their lives. We began inviting them into fellowship and exposing them to American culture, sharing baby showers, weddings, memorials, picnics, slip and slides, and college football. But there's also much dignity in allowing the other party to give back. Friendship is reciprocal. Knowing that several Burmese friends had become skilled in making sushi, for my wife's birthday I threw a roll-your-own-sushi party. I invited our Burmese friends Sam and Kyau Kim and humbly told them, "I need your help. We need to learn from you. Could you teach us this skill?" And we all got to share a meal. Mostly, I needed help and had to learn to receive it. Since then, our church has hosted several roll-your-own-sushi nights in different homes. It gives us a way to dignify our friendships, listen to their stories, and invite neighbors to experience what an active faith and community might look like.

What's evident is that this kind of reciprocal hospitality bears witness to the heart of God. Relationships are not random. Connecting with people, even strangers, is never an accident. These are divine appointments, even if God never enters the conversation. What hope of heaven can you bring to friends, neighbors, clients, coworkers, acquaintances, family, and strangers through hospitality?

Sometimes, you might be called on to give of yourself. Other times, you might need to receive, even if it's for the other person's benefit as much as for yours. Our capacity to receive is not just about deepening human relationships. It's also how we're able to grow spiritually in the grace of God.

Through the story of a foreigner who was both well educated and confused, Acts 8 highlights how hospitality creates disciples (Acts 8:26-40). The man, an Ethiopian eunuch and court official, had traveled to Jerusalem to worship at the Temple. Perhaps he had heard of the Jewish God, Yahweh, and was curious. But when he got there, he probably would have been reminded of his outsider status, since as a Gentile, he would not have been permitted to enter the inner areas of the Temple.

Let's just pause here. Have you ever been on the outside looking in? Have you ever been made to feel like others are thinking, *You're not one of us*? Have you ever been dismissed or disqualified because you didn't fit? In this story in Acts 8, we find a black man from Africa visiting Jerusalem. He was spiritually hungry but theologically starved. He was wealthy, well-traveled, educated, and a CFO for a queen . . . *and yet*, among the people of God, he was an outsider! He's just come from the Temple, which has five courts that create physical and spiritual barriers for participation.[1] What's more, being in the queen's service meant becoming a eunuch (see Deuteronomy 23:1). So when this Ethiopian finds Philip, he's ushered into the gospel, God's presence, and the outworking of heaven on earth . . . and it changes his life.

The redemptive power of the gospel is about making room, removing barriers, and overcoming division. Imagine traveling to another continent to seek this God. Hospitality goes a long way as an expression of faith. Our ability to make room and receive blessing from someone seemingly different from ourselves is one of the most significant witnesses a Christian can practice. And thankfully, the apostle Philip answered this call.

The Lord told Philip to head down the desert road. He obeyed, and soon he crossed paths with the Ethiopian man, whom he could hear reading the Bible aloud. Philip received an invitation to join him in his chariot. Stepping up to the seat, Philip asked the Ethiopian if he understood what he was reading, to which the man replied, "How can I . . . unless someone explains it to me?" (Acts 8:31). He was reading the Scriptures, but he needed help understanding. Clearly God had prepared this man's heart for Philip to host. And He does the same thing for every Christ follower!

MAKING FAITH AND COMMUNITY ACCESSIBLE

Of course, this doesn't mean that hospitality is always easy. The story of the Ethiopian man illustrates this as well. He knew that central to being Jewish is the practice of circumcision. That's a significant problem for this Ethiopian *because he's a eunuch!* This is where Philip was incredibly accommodating. We're told that the Ethiopian was reading Isaiah 53 and asked Philip to explain it to him. Philip would have been familiar with the context of this chapter and chapter 56, which give a clear picture of prophetic and redemptive hope. Imagine this Ethiopian, after what he had just experienced in the Temple courts, reading these words:

> Let no foreigner who is bound to the LORD say,
>   "The LORD will surely exclude me from his people."
> And let no eunuch complain,
>   "I am only a dry tree."

> For this is what the LORD says:

> "To the eunuchs who keep my Sabbaths,
>   who choose what pleases me

and hold fast to my covenant—
to them I will give within my temple and its walls
    a memorial and a name
    better than sons and daughters;
I will give them an everlasting name
    that will endure forever."

ISAIAH 56:3-5

For the eunuch, Christian hospitality made God's love seem more accessible. Once a cultural and religious outsider, he gained full acceptance into a community of faith. That's good news! This made faith more compelling than any amount of riches, education, or class standing could afford him.

The gospel was always supposed to be the vehicle to cross social divides. Instead of dividing, the gospel can unify people regardless of gender, culture, race, education, or social class. To complete the experience, when the Ethiopian eunuch saw some water, he asked to be baptized. The Ethiopian understood that, in contrast to his previous inability to convert to the Jewish faith, he was now welcomed as a member of this new Jesus movement! This is hospitality as evangelism. Making room. Learning to follow. Proclaiming the Good News.

It's interesting to ask who this story is about, the Ethiopian or Philip. At first glance, it seems to be about the eunuch coming to faith and then wanting to be baptized. But what if the author, Luke, wants you to see the everyday Christian life of being sent into the world?

Philip was open to opportunities. That didn't make him an expert. But here's what is true: The more I put myself in situations that require God's wisdom and strength, the more I realize that His power is made perfect in my weakness (2 Corinthians 12:9).

I've also found the more I encounter delicate problems, the more comforting, encouraging, and poised I become. But it is always intimidating to start; I often feel underqualified. If you want to grow spiritually, be willing to put yourself into roles and situations that require faith.

ORDINARY HOSPITALITY

A new phase of Jesus' ministry began when He sent the apostles to do the preaching, teaching, and healing they had observed Him doing. Initially, Jesus traveled with the four fishermen. Later, seventy-two were with Him, and He sent them out in pairs. There had been a lot of observing, instructing, demonstrating, and debriefing. Before Jesus gave the great commission, He experimented with what it meant to live on mission. That is, learning to live not just as believers but as "sent ones." The way He did it was by teaching the disciples about hospitality. We see Jesus' strategy of ordinary hospitality in the sending of the seventy-two:

> After this the Lord appointed seventy-two others and
> sent them two by two ahead of him to every town and
> place where he was about to go. He told them, "The
> harvest is plentiful, but the workers are few. Ask the
> Lord of the harvest, therefore, to send out workers into
> his harvest field. Go! I am sending you out like lambs
> among wolves. Do not take a purse or bag or sandals;
> and do not greet anyone on the road.
>
> "When you enter a house, first say, 'Peace to this

house.' If someone who promotes peace is there, your peace will rest on them; if not, it will return to you. Stay there, eating and drinking whatever they give you, for the worker deserves his wages. Do not move around from house to house.

"When you enter a town and are welcomed, eat what is offered to you. Heal the sick who are there and tell them, 'The kingdom of God has come near to you.'"

LUKE 10:1-9

Jesus paints a new picture of what it means to follow.

No longer would the disciples simply gather in the Temple or stay within the comfort of their small groups. They were to go out. Jesus gave them His power and authority and marching orders. He sends them to find those spiritually curious. After His resurrection, He would send them to every people group in every place. In this training exercise, they were to take no provisions—no money, spare sandals, food, extra coat—nor were they to get too comfortable, being sent "like lambs among wolves." But they were encouraged to look for people who showed them kindness.

We tend to interpret the favor we receive from others as if it's about our personality, resources, looks, and connections—and it could very well be. But the more we see our lives *in Christ*, the more we understand how God draws others to His Son *through us*! When we live on mission—as sent ones of God—we realize that our chief aim is to point others closer to Jesus. Again, the goal is to identify whom God has prepared for us and be able to share the difference with them that Christ makes in us. That is what discipleship is all about.

From this Scripture, it is reasonable to conclude that we also have people of peace in our lives today and that you are someone else's person of peace. God has been preparing you in advance to help or receive help from someone, or to share the Good News with someone. The question is always *How will you use that influence?*

Our job isn't to have all the correct answers, the perfect approach, or even to be convincing. Our job is simply to let the Spirit lead whom the Spirit has prepared. Start with an invitation to coffee, a meal, or a conversation. Have a conversation and see where it goes! Our job is not to find converts. Our mission is to help people take the next steps in faith toward Christ.

DISCUSSION QUESTIONS

1. How is the rhythm of hospitality an outward expression of faith? Is there an analogy or metaphor that could help you digest it personally and communicate it?

2. Have you ever been "interrupted" by a need to help someone you hardly knew? We are confronted with needs and requests all the time. What was it about this compelling need that made it stand out?

3. Can you name a person with whom you've had the chance to get close, yet he or she is different from you? Consider disparities in age, life stage, culture, economics, education, and race. Describe the circumstances that helped you bond.

Finding Your Rhythm

Discerning Whom God Has
Prepared in Advance for You

THE GREAT COMMISSION in Matthew 28—Jesus' command to make disciples—was given to the Eleven, but it's generally understood to apply to all followers of Jesus who come after them. All believers are included in this commission, not just pastors and missionaries. Jesus offers few prayer requests. In the Luke 10 passage, it's for laborers for the harvest. A laborer knows how to discern whom God has prepared and how to connect with them. Then, Jesus becomes part of the answer to the prayer in sending out the next round of disciples.

Read Luke 10:1-17. A meaningful response to the great commission is helping others take their next steps in their relationship with Christ *through you*. Living with a sense of mission means learning to see people and opportunities that we can respond to—at least in small part—in our daily lives.

DISCOVERING WHOM GOD HAS PREPARED FOR YOU

Ultimately, a practice of hospitality, whether on the giving or receiving end, is about discerning whom God has prepared in advance for us. In the next month, **pray and identify people who welcome, serve, or listen to you.** These people ask for your help and advice or offer hospitality. These people are spiritual but not necessarily Christian. They're willing to serve but not yet part of a church family. They might have doubts or questions or have been hurt by the church, yet they seem to show you favor and influence.

What questions are they asking that you could help answer? What kind of activity could you include them in (participating in a small group, attending church, hanging out with friends, or volunteering together)?

Make it your goal to identify five "people of peace." Try to hear their stories. Is there a need? What's their gift? In what way can you encourage, support, or receive from them? Share this list with a trusted friend or fellow disciplemaker and begin including them in your regular prayers.

-
-
-
-
-

PROCLAIMING THE KINGDOM OF GOD TO THEM

The Good News is much more than having our sins forgiven while on earth and then going to heaven when we die. Inviting someone to surrender their life to Christ is about God's passionate desire to restore the world. Aligning our lives with Christ allows us to become cocreators and divine participants in the world that God intended and will fully restore when Christ returns!

When Jesus sent the disciples, it was to share the Good News. More than simply believing the right things and convincing people to say the proper prayers, they were to share the difference Christ was making in their lives. This personal testimony wouldn't be debatable; it would also be (I hope) evident in their speech and conduct.

An essential aspect of bearing witness or sharing the Good News is describing the difference Christ is making in you. Every testimony involves three elements: *before I met Christ, how I met Christ*, and *since I met Christ*. (The third element tends to be most compelling to the spiritually curious.) As we find ways to talk about the difference Christ is making in us, it gives us confidence to share in real and personal ways.

Write out your faith story in three parts. Your primary objectives in writing and memorizing your testimony are to better relate to the average, spiritually curious person and to share, clearly and concisely, how you came to know Christ. The questions below can help frame your story. (Pro tip: When shared, your story only needs to last three to four minutes.)

Part 1: Before I Knew Christ

What was my life like when I lived for personal success and interest?

What did my life revolve around? From what source did I derive my happiness, worth, or security?

How did those things let me down or fail to satisfy me? (Describe how you felt a void in your life before you knew Christ.)

Part 2: How I Aligned My Life with Christ's

When was the first time I heard the gospel? (Think about when you saw true Christianity being lived out or when you first understood that God intended something better for this world.)

When did my attitude, desires, and motivation begin to change? Why?

What excites me about aligning with God's heart for justice, mercy, renewal, and hope?

Part 3: Since I Arranged My Life in Christ

What specific changes has Christ made in my life? Are there any illustrations that help describe my change of heart? How am I motivated differently now than I was before I knew Christ?

What causes or concerns have I discovered or developed due to growing in Christ?

Is there a Bible verse that I hold close as a trusted promise?

4

THE RHYTHM OF
COMMUNITY

Discovering Your Potential and Finding Your Contribution

Love each other with genuine affection, and
take delight in honoring each other.
ROMANS 12:10, NLT

IT'S NOT QUITE A BUMPER STICKER YET, but *We make awkward look effortless!* has become a rallying cry within our community whenever we experience a steep learning curve together.

The reason it's okay is that we're awkward together, which is much better than being awkward by yourself. When I remind people of our rhythm of community, it draws a smile and bonds us together as we jointly work out our faith and mission. There's nothing like going through some new, strange, and stretching experience among friends. Have you ever been on a cross-cultural trip or visited homes in a less industrialized country? Ever sat with a person experiencing homelessness who's battling mental illness? Or found yourself trying to care for a recent immigrant while culture and language keep getting in the way? It's not easy, but it's a bonding experience.

Something happens when a group of people who are curious about expressing faith and concerned about the vulnerable and marginalized choose to be uncomfortable or inconvenienced together. This is critical to understand because it reflects the strength of Christian community. The church exists as a missional expression of the Kingdom of God on earth, and your approach to this expression matters. If you start with being in community as a goal (i.e., a life-stage group, shared activity, or even a worship service), you rarely end up on mission. But if you start with being on mission together, you always end up in community.

Disciplemaking has much to do with orienting our relationships missionally (that is, to keep us focused on living as "sent ones"). Disciples learn how mission transcends age and life stage because we're gathered for something beyond self-interest. When a person pushes beyond their own comfort level by faith, it's hard to sustain the motivation to keep going or to do it again. However, when they feel the support and encouragement of a community to practice faith in tangible ways, individuals are more likely to thrive. When a group goes through challenges together for the sake of others, bonds are forged, and real change happens.

As a disciplemaker, your greatest impact is in helping someone realize their potential. In this context, apprenticing means learning to find one's contribution within the community of faith. Again, a faith community is much like a family whose members divide the chores. It isn't always fun, but it is good to be part of the group. It's a way we invest in each other, demonstrate care, and serve God.

Small-batch disciplemaking doesn't stop with those you know, like, or care about. We see in the early New Testament church that community worked because of proximity and intentionality. In other words, they had a standing appointment that allowed Christ followers to develop and expand (Acts 2:42). The believers were around each other long enough to know each other's needs, share their resources, serve each other, pray together, hold each other accountable, and work to include others outside the community.

Western culture values independence. We like to show up, give, and help on our own terms. But what if the most significant way God wants to change us is by having us become *inter*dependent? That's not something we can do on our own.

SEEING THE POTENTIAL IN OTHERS

It seems foreign to disciple someone into community, so let's ask the question differently. Who modeled for you what it meant to be family? Even if your family of origin was dysfunctional, you can probably think of someone who went out of their way to make you feel welcome, was self-sacrificial, was loyal, or otherwise revealed the greater good of a group. Since many marriages and families have broken down and dissolved, we need to help people reimagine the life-changing role Christian community plays in the life of a believer. And the best way to learn (or unlearn) what it means to be in community is through an apprenticing relationship.

What if we imagine a rhythm of community as being similar to blood circulation? In extreme physical conditions, much of our blood retreats to the vital organs. Things like shivering and frostbite or dehydration and lightheadedness occur when circulation changes in response to extreme temperatures.

Under extreme spiritual conditions, where do we retreat spiritually? Into greater sin or surrender? Isolation or interdependence? Community is the mechanism God uses to remind us of what's true (who we are in light of who He is) and to show us that we're not alone, that there's a better way. But true community requires more than similar interests, shared history, or common activities. It calls us to pursue people who are further along in their faith journey and to invite others to follow. It's about proximity and intentionality. It involves defining an inner circle of people who are emotionally and spiritually healthy and investing in them as if your life depends on it . . . because it just might. The power of this kind of community is that we are able to see—and act on behalf of—another's potential.

An unusual story of the power of community came from the 2006 Winter Olympics. Competing in a thirty-kilometer (eighteen-mile) race, which I watched with my family, Frode Estil, a Norwegian cross-country skier, was heavily favored to win. At the starting line, though, Estil got tangled up in the fury of the pack all vying for position as the gun went off. Instead of being able to find a manageable place and pace to execute his race strategy, he fell, got trampled, and broke a ski. In a field of seventy-six skiers, the favored Estil was dead last and couldn't continue. But he was able to find replacement equipment quickly. And finally, he was off, now forty-five seconds behind the leader. And this is where we're reminded that—regardless of how individually talented we are—we're simply better together. The team stepped up. Aware of Estil's fall, two teammates expended extra energy to climb their way to the front of the pack and controlled the pace of the entire field, slowing it down enough to give their teammate a chance to catch up. Despite the setback, Estil worked his way back into contention. Of course, his teammates couldn't sustain their pace and never placed in the race, but Estil won the silver medal, missing the gold by 1.6 seconds!

It's interesting to reflect on this story from different vantage points. We can look at it from that of a fallen friend who won't give up. We might view it as teammates who see the potential of a gifted athlete. We can see it from the view of a competitor with a burning desire to win. And still, we also might observe it as a helpless spectator paralyzed to help beyond cheers, admiration, or prayers. The beauty of this story is that few people recall who finished that race first. Second place was the most significant victory that day. The story is about overcoming challenging and potentially devastating circumstances. And the secret to overcoming, for Estil in that race and for us today, is the community of people we surround ourselves with.

The people closest to us can see our potential, sometimes better than we see it ourselves. In this case, these Norwegian skiers had trained together and competed to the point where they knew what each other was capable of. How does this apply to disciplemaking? Failure wouldn't feel like failure if we knew we weren't alone in the attempt. What if we're already predisposed to help another person grow in service, develop their gifts, and find their voice while also discerning God's? Life is most meaningful when we compete for the success of another person. This is why parenting brings both immeasurable joy and profound heartache. Parenting, by nature, requires us to invest in the success of someone else. But what if this strategy isn't limited to the confines of parenting? What if another person's spiritual potential is part of the DNA of a small group? What if being part of the church community means being committed to developmental relationships? Might our feelings of failure dwindle?

In *Bread for the Journey*, Henri Nouwen wrote, "Community is first of all a quality of the heart. It grows from the spiritual knowledge that we are alive not for ourselves but for one another. Community is the fruit of our capacity to make the interests of others more important than our own (see Philippians 2:4). The question, therefore, is not 'How can we make community?' but 'How can we develop and nurture giving hearts?'"[1]

What we learn is that the biblical community never works as an end in itself. By the fourth century, the churches in Rome were feeding an estimated twenty thousand poor people each week. The church at that time presented to the world a visible alternative to the prevailing social order. As theologian and historian Georges Florovsky wrote in an essay on Christian history:

> Christianity entered history as a new social order, or
> rather a new social dimension. From the very beginning
> Christianity was not primarily a "doctrine," but exactly
> a "community." There was not only a "Message" to
> be proclaimed and delivered, and "Good News" to
> be declared. There was precisely a New Community,

distinct and peculiar, in the process of growth and
formation, to which members were called and recruited.
Indeed, "fellowship" (*koinonia*) was the basic category
of Christian existence.[2]

Again, if you start with building community, you rarely find
a mission. If you start with a shared mission, you always find
community. If a person simply attends church on Sundays, they
might be inspired, but they will miss the impact. They might be
encouraged, but it is unlikely they will be transformed. Impact
occurs when we're willing to wade deeply into relationships and
ministry. This understanding of community is vital for a realistic expectation of what God and the local church can do.

FAITH AS A FAMILY AFFAIR

A few years ago, a famous Christian author stirred the pot when
he announced he didn't want or need to go to church anymore.
The negative reaction wasn't just about poor stewardship of
his influence as a Christian leader; the objection was based on
the biblical notion that we are not to give up on church: "not
giving up meeting together, as some are in the habit of doing"
(Hebrews 10:25). The author provided his rebuttal, which I
didn't fully agree with—however, something he wrote really
stuck with me.

He said that the church has always mirrored institutions
that secular culture would understand and relate to. He
described how in the Middle Ages, the church reflected the
government hierarchy, from the pope to cardinals to bishops
to priests on down, which was viewed as a source of protection

and provision. After the invention of the Gutenberg Press and the Age of Enlightenment, the church became an educational institution. Churches reflected classrooms with a primarily knowledge-based approach to discipleship. And for the past thirty years, the Protestant church has resembled the entertainment industry, with rock bands, slick videos, attempts at drama, and light shows. His simple point was that he didn't attend church because he didn't want to be entertained. While I felt like this author's public declaration may have been a ploy to grab attention, I agreed with one point: The church has always attempted—for better or for worse—to mirror something that our culture could understand and relate to. Attracting crowds isn't a bad thing, but it can be a spiritually limiting dynamic if people stop there. Let's celebrate their curiosity and willingness to step inside.

The writer didn't provide an alternative to church mirroring the entertainment culture, but it got me thinking: *What are people hungry for that could impact people more today? What is something that people outside the church long for and relate to?*

After a couple weeks of wondering, it came to me: *family.*

It seemed so simple and obvious. As our culture has seen the increasing disintegration of marriage and the demise of the nuclear family, we've also lost the enduring presence and stability of the extended family.

The rhythm of community is about adopting a stronger commitment to contributing and discovering our potential, as we would in a family. And this takes practice! It takes work to be together and to be supportive, sacrificial, forgiving, and gracious. But it also helps us experience God's love and participate with grace. In a dynamic Christian community, the sum is always more potent than the parts.

For millennia, society was impacted by the nuclear family functioning as a cornerstone with the extended family supporting it. Today, we have not only lost the formative influence of the extended family but also seen the nuclear family break down and dissolve. In ancient Israel, when it was time for a man and woman to marry, the young man would prepare a place for them by building a new house adjacent to his father's existing one. Sometimes it would be an upper room with an external staircase. As generations married and built their homes onto the original ones, they created a housing complex called an insula— a cluster of multilevel buildings where extended families lived around a central courtyard. Grandparents, cousins, uncles, and aunts all lived in community. As the son worked on his new home, he awaited his father's final approval.

The family metaphor is interesting, especially as it relates to being in the church and growing in faith. Although not everyone in ancient Israel lived communally like this, many people did. The insula (think: insulation) was a compound-like structure where additional rooms were added for growing families and children beginning their own nuclear families. It was where generations came to understand that one's problems, parents, or resources weren't theirs alone. In an insula, there's collective wisdom and the safety of being known without fearing rejection. When a marriage struggles, there's someone who's been married longer who can share from their experience. Other influential adults can echo the same message when parents feel they are losing their authority or influence over their kids.

*The insula, or church, is the place where we make each
other better.
And the insula works well when everyone is able to
contribute.*

*Everyone shares in the joys and responsibilities. Everyone carries
the concern and the success.* With this extended-family system
came built-in authority, training, mentoring, and support. The
idea that "it takes a village" was real. Historically, this environment was how children were raised, marriages were nurtured,
and the elderly were honored, sought after, and cared for. It
was where values were impressed, beliefs were taught, traditions were observed, and a family trade was learned. Whatever
stage of life you were in, others could always offer support in
matters of marriage, parenting, finances, and faith. Like any
family environment, the expectation of its members was for
shared responsibility. There was an expectation to learn, give,
and help for the collective good. By nature of proximity and
close relationship, the investment in the next generation was
clear, whether in the family trade or the oral tradition. The
values, beliefs, and skills were to be passed down.

Think about it. We live in a society with profound authority issues, but everyone needs the trusted wisdom of
people who have experience the rest of us lack. Particularly in
the Western world, we need people who have been married
longer, raised kids well, walked with Jesus further, endured
hardship, overcome adversity, buried their parents, and don't
feel like they need to be heard or have the last word. The
church has such a fantastic opportunity to be for our culture

exactly what the culture needs and lacks—*an extended family of faith*!

I relate to this picture of an extended family of faith because, in many ways, it resembles my church experience growing up in San Francisco. Ours was a nondenominational church, mostly blue-collar, in the Mission District—a diverse and densely populated neighborhood largely of South and Central American immigrants. The church was made up of many first- and second-generation immigrants, which beautifully reflected the city's diversity, with over fifty nations represented. In the late 1980s, the church averaged around four hundred people in attendance, which felt large for an evangelical church within the city. What made my experience there especially unique was that, despite growing up in this urban and mobile context, both of my parents' families attended the church. I had aunts and uncles on my mom's side who were friends with family on my dad's side. Many, like my mom, came to the US after the Nazi occupation of Scandinavia. The church became their extended family.

There was an elder in the church who had immigrated from Sweden years before my mom. On my mom's first day of middle school, this elder went to the school with my grandma and mom to translate for them and help them settle in. Also in our church were a half-dozen contractors willing to hire immigrants who wanted to learn a trade. If you needed something—help with your car, a remodel on your house, a haircut, wedding flowers, a seamstress, or family Christmas photos—there was someone at the church who could help. Like the insula of ancient Israel, ours was a church with intergenerational relationships able to teach a trade, support a fragile marriage, explain Bible passages, or come alongside weary parents. There were volunteer youth leaders to echo the same message of God's relentless love. There were young adults to hold the youth accountable. A volunteer culture operated as the hub for help and support. It was the ultimate picture of an extended family of faith. Pastors came and went but what always remained was the community of faith. Since the church ran primarily on the backs of servant-hearted saints, this wasn't merely a church with content to consume. Rather, it was many parts of one body doing Kingdom work.

CREATED FOR COMMUNITY

Community seems like too much of a buzzword. Many places advertise it, and it feels like it's all around us, at least on some level. We have an office-workroom community, a neighborhood community, and a carpooling community. We have a youth-sports community, social-media community, and a happy-hour community. We have familiar faces at church, the gym, our neighborhood, and our regular coffee spot. Why is it that though we've never been more connected, we feel so isolated, lonely, and disconnected? We need people actively present in our lives.

We don't usually think of a "practicing" community. What's there to practice? You either see someone or you don't. Like them or not. Yet community is more than simply finding someone pleasant, agreeing with them, having the same socioeconomic status, or enjoying some of the same things. One way to think about forming a more substantial concept of community is by thinking of it as what author and activist Parker Palmer calls "the place where the person you least want to live with always lives."[3] Henri Nouwen described this robust kind of biblical community as "where your childhood of God is constantly put through the mill of human relationships. . . . Community is a place where Judas always is and sometimes it is just you."[4] Finding the right church is more than finding others in the same life stage. It's more than simply seeing familiar faces. It's more than having a history together. Community is discovering what we have in common with others—specifically, people who are seemingly *unlike* us—merely because we all bear the image of God.

In our Western culture, we often end up shopping at a church like it's a mall full of religious goods and services. People like sitting anonymously, especially in larger churches, without much notice, participation, or contribution. Of course, everyone needs time to feel comfortable. But it's much easier to show up or skip without anyone noticing. Remaining anonymous keeps us from any meaningful ownership of the relationships or the actual work of the ministry. And without this kind of ownership, churches are primarily left to produce spiritual consumers. Unfortunately, personal consumption never leads to transformation. What's more, we've largely made discipleship about knowledge without mission. Never has great faith teaching been more readily available through digital services. But listening to faith-based podcasts and audiobooks on our commute can't replace the role that mission and community are meant to have in the lives of Christ followers.

The practice of community involves discovering what we

have in common despite our apparent differences. It's not something we create. Community is what we find when we're willing and able to put the time and effort into relationships. This is the answer to our prayer *Your will be done, on earth as it is in heaven.* Who among us hasn't come to appreciate a neighbor or coworker simply because circumstances forced us into proximity with them?

Humans' need for community is revealed in the very beginning of the Bible, in the creation story. What does God say about our image? "Let *us* make mankind in *our* image" (Genesis 1:26, emphasis added). God is inherently a relational God who exists in a community. We see a kind of fellowship within God's trinity—and a need for fellowship within our own nature. Genesis 2:18 says, "It is not good for the man [humans] to be alone." Our relational needs are central to being human, not just to being Christian. Before we were introduced to sin, before the devil appeared, God said that it's not good for people to be alone. In other words, *we were created to know and be known by others.* This truth explains why people from different walks of life can find points of interest and connection. It's interesting to note that man wasn't alone. God walked with Adam and Eve "in the cool of the day" (Genesis 3:8). But when God said, "It is not good for the man to be alone," He wasn't discounting His presence; He was referring to other humans. In other words, it's not good for man to be without another of the same kind. God made us with the need for other image bearers. One very practical application to consider is that every introvert is actually better off when they find a discipline for relational, even group, participation and engagement. Similarly, extroverts benefit from deliberate times of solitude, silence, and contemplation. The point is that God is found in both settings and is meant to be experienced and enjoyed in each. So to limit oneself to one or the other actually can limit the Spirit's work within our hearts, minds, bodies, and relationships.

A SACRAMENTAL TRIBE

It's fun to get dressed up for a wedding, enjoy good food, and have a dance party. But I like to remind people that weddings are more than spectator events. The privilege of a wedding invitation reveals a level of appreciation and connection. And marriages need support. So when I officiate a wedding, I like to point out to all the guests that their presence means their "I dos" to support this couple in keeping their vows. Being in the community should encourage us to pray for and encourage the couple, finding ways to help lighten their load when life's challenges become burdensome. Things like marriage, parenting, and faith are always better as team sports, as they were intended to be. In other words, we're not supposed to attempt these things without a supporting cast. This is the power of community.

Similarly, when parents bring their children to be dedicated, it's a reminder to the congregation that it takes a church to raise a child. Dedicating a child to God acknowledges God's authority over the child and their mom and dad. Parents present their children before God and His people, asking for grace and wisdom in their parenting responsibilities. Parents also pray that their child might one day align their life with Jesus. Sometimes our kids make us look like much better parents than we really are. Other times, they can make us look like worse parents than we are. The truth probably lies somewhere in the middle! The point is that Christian parents can thrive within a biblical community willing to echo the same message of God's love, the same boundaries, and the same purity in speech and teaching. Therefore, the church is at its best when people answer the call to love one another—to say "I do" to the community—by serving other parents in children's and youth ministries.

Getting baptized is another "I do" within the Christian community. We baptize publicly to show a believer's personal desire and commitment to follow Christ. Paul wrote to the Roman church, "We were therefore buried with him through baptism into death in order that, just as Christ was raised from the dead through the glory of the Father, we too may live a new life" (Romans 6:4). While baptism is individually administered, it is also a communal act. When one of us suffers, we all suffer. When one of us rejoices, we celebrate with them. So when a person is at an age and stage to identify with the life, death, and resurrection of Christ, they need an intentional community. Whenever a person makes strides in faith, they're making themselves vulnerable to spiritual attacks. The kingdom of darkness is constantly threatened by our walking in obedience. This is where the presence of the Holy Spirit is needed most. And the place that the Spirit primarily manifests is in the saints who are already in proximity.

What if we begin to approach church membership as a covenant? Specifically, the church invites people into a covenant with Jesus through their church family. But rather than inviting people to a static, one-time commitment, we invite people to renew their vow to God and the church yearly. Life stages, work demands, and personal circumstances change yearly. At our church, we encourage people to consider actively—in January each year—how they follow Christ within the faith community. As New Year's resolutions go, I have never heard of anyone deciding to grow in love, which is the point. As we noted while discussing the rhythm of apprenticing, we simply can't self-help our way to transformation. In other words, transformation is communal. Community is not hard to find if we simply define it as familiar faces or shared interests. But a *faith* community shares belief in a living God and a shared practice of faith! We can make decisions on our own, but to sustain changes, we need to surround ourselves with people to stand in solidarity with and people who might be further along in Christian mission and formation.

REFRAMING ADOPTION

Coming of age spiritually, as we learn to trust in Christ, is not unlike how the adoption process was viewed in the early church. Understanding our spiritual adoption as God's sons and daughters can similarly have a life-changing effect on our perspective of how we experience salvation and grow in faith.

Once we put our faith in Christ, we are adopted as God's sons and daughters.

Paul writes to a group of new Christians in Galatia about coming of age spiritually (Galatians 4:1-7). He contrasts an underage heir with a slave. We tend to think that being a child of God means we're helpless and only able to receive. Adoption in Scripture, however, means accepting the privileges and responsibilities of a full-grown heir. In other words, God adopts or saves us with the idea that we grow and mature into trusted contributors to God's salvation on earth.

In his book *Becoming Who God Intended*, David Eckman highlights "a critical difference between the ancient world and the modern world. In the ancient world, they rarely adopted babies, but instead they adopted adults. . . . When a childless couple was getting so old that any possibility of child-bearing was gone, if well-off, they would legally adopt a young man whom they loved and trusted to take over the family business and handle the family wealth. This was so the couple would be taken care of in their old age."[5] Similarly, God has placed us in a family—with Christ—and wants us to live with a new identity. We are invited to come of age as trusted heirs! Our heavenly Father looks to adopt us, but not as helpless, consuming children. Instead, we're invited to be valued contributors to the Father's business. In this case, the church isn't a service you attend but a service you offer to one another in the same way you'd serve your family.

DISCUSSION QUESTIONS

1. How do you think a faith community (i.e., being part of a church) is *ideally* different from a book club, running group, parents of kids on the same sports team, or even people living in the same neighborhood?

2. In familiar group settings, are you more comfortable having a task, sharing an activity, or hosting a

conversation? What does this preference suggest to you about possible roles for you in your faith community?

3. Who in your community—those with whom you regularly socialize with—falls outside your life stage, education level, or ethnic background? Can you identify a character quality or other adjective that describes how your relationship with this person adds value to your life?

4. Can you name someone who saw your potential and worked with you to develop it?

5. This chapter posed three metaphors for biblical community—as blood circulation, as an extended family, and as a marriage covenant with renewable vows. Which one resonates most with you? How would you describe your experience of biblical community using this metaphor?

Finding Your Rhythm

Called to Be "With-nesses":
The Practice of Intentional Faith in Community

THE NAME IMMANUEL MEANS "God with us." In this sense, God's middle name is *with*. So who are your "with-nesses"? Who are the pilgrims in proximity to you with whom you can be the person God has called you to be? Everyone is relational in their own way, but not everyone understands how to be "in community." Of course, people are wired differently—some feed off other people's energy, while others need quiet, solitude, or downtime to recharge. Yet we're all created relationally because we bear the image of a relational God. In many cases, the spiritual practice for introverts requires finding a discipline for engagement with others. Extroverts need discipline for quiet solitude and reflection. In either case, a rhythm for engaging in community is necessary to grow in Christ.

THE "ONE ANOTHER" PHRASES

Teaching us how to be a faith community, the New Testament gives over fifty "one another" phrases outlining a clear picture of the commitment involved. **Read through the passages below** and consider how many of these commands can be fulfilled in a worship service versus how many occur beyond it.[6]

1. "Be devoted to *one another* in love. Honor *one another* above yourselves" (Romans 12:10).
2. "Live in harmony with *one another*. Do not be proud, but be willing to associate with people of low position" (Romans 12:16).
3. "Let no debt remain outstanding, except the continuing debt to love *one another*, for whoever loves others has fulfilled the law" (Romans 13:8).
4. "Stop passing judgment on *one another*. Instead, make up your mind not to put any stumbling block or obstacle in the way of a brother or sister" (Romans 14:13).
5. "Accept *one another*, then, just as Christ accepted you" (Romans 15:7).
6. "Instruct *one another*" (Romans 15:14).
7. "Serve *one another* humbly in love" (Galatians 5:13).
8. "Carry *each other's* burdens, and in this way you will fulfill the law of Christ" (Galatians 6:2).

9. "Be completely humble and gentle; be patient, bearing with *one another* in love" (Ephesians 4:2).

10. "Be kind and compassionate to *one another*, forgiving each other, just as in Christ God forgave you" (Ephesians 4:32).

11. "Bear with each other and forgive *one another* if any of you has a grievance against someone" (Colossians 3:13).

12. "Teach and admonish *one another* with all wisdom through psalms, hymns, and songs from the Spirit, singing to God with gratitude in your hearts" (Colossians 3:16).

13. "Encourage *one another* and build each other up" (1 Thessalonians 5:11).

14. "Live in peace with *one another*" (1 Thessalonians 5:13, NASB).

15. "Spur *one another* on toward love and good deeds" (Hebrews 10:24).

16. "Confess your sins to *each other* and pray for each other so that you may be healed" (James 5:16).

17. "Be like-minded, be sympathetic, love *one another*, be compassionate and humble" (1 Peter 3:8).

18. "Offer hospitality to *one another* without grumbling" (1 Peter 4:9).

19. "Clothe yourselves with humility toward *one another*" (1 Peter 5:5).

20. "Have fellowship with *one another*" (1 John 1:7).

The question is: *What does God have in mind for a biblical community?* The church needs right belief (orthodoxy), but the church also needs right practice (orthopraxy). Knowledge alone, without mission, incarnation, or (notably) spiritual reproduction is not effective for God's work in the world, much less in Christian hearts. It's about right doctrine and "with-ness." Church is more than attending a weekly service; it's also being relationally committed to a community of believers.

Paul, writing to Philemon (a church leader hosting the church in his home), uses key descriptors to celebrate the kind of community they maintain. From this, we get a better idea of what church is supposed to look like, mean, and require.

> This letter is from Paul, a prisoner for preaching the Good News about Christ Jesus, and from our brother Timothy.
>
> I am writing to Philemon, our beloved co-worker, and to our sister Apphia, and to our fellow soldier Archippus, and to the church that meets in your house.
>
> May God our Father and the Lord Jesus Christ give you grace and peace.
>
> PHILEMON 1:1-3, NLT

Notice the words *co-worker, fellow soldier, meets in your house.*
Answer the following questions.

1. Who are the people closest to you who are the healthiest, spiritually and emotionally? Whose faces come to mind when you think about how your faith is growing? Who are your co-workers for the sake of the gospel?

2. Whose back are you watching, like that of a "fellow soldier"?

3. When meeting together for worship, service, or small group, whose absence do you notice? Who comes to mind as someone who might benefit from—and be open to—more of an apprenticing relationship with you?

YOUR APPRENTICING COMMUNITY

Take a 360-degree inventory of the influences in your life. This exercise is designed to help you see the larger network that makes up a developmental community. Community is more than just familiar faces at the gym, in the neighborhood, at work, or in our book clubs. You're looking to identify the specific people who stimulate you to grow in Christ.

Who keeps you from making the same mistake twice? Who is current with what's going on in your life? Who says no to your yes without burning a bridge? Who are you training with to run the marathon of life? We can't just try to run a marathon without training first. The same principle is true with faith if we want to experience life to its fullest.

Take a little time to write down two or three names of people who might fit the following categories. Again, these people should mostly be within proximity of your life and current with your circumstances. Don't try to complete this in one sitting. Let it simmer over the next week. Come back to it three to four times. I'd also encourage you to pray Psalm 139, especially the first few verses. Read it slowly, waiting for any impressions of names and faces. Allow the Holy Spirit to bring revelation.

Models: people you look up to and admire (who you may or may not know personally)

-
-
-

Mentors: people who coach and/or invest in you (either presently or in your past)

-
-
-

Inner circle: those closest to you (think of the ones who are the healthiest, emotionally and spiritually, ideally those who live locally and with whom you're able to receive accountability.)

-
-
-

Followers: people you lead

-
-
-

Apprentices: people you are investing in (either formally or informally)

-
-
-

People of peace: those you are seeking to lead closer to Christ

-
-
-

Foes: people you are at odds with who are still part of your life. These are people you tend to avoid being around. It might also be helpful to name the offense that's created a rift.

-
-
-

Over the next two weeks, choose at least one of these suggested community-building ideas to practice individually, in your apprenticing, or within a small group:

- Get to know the deeper story of each other's lives, particularly those of individuals from another life stage, background, and/or experience.

- Be part of a weekly ministry team that serves your church family in some way. Remember, this is part of your "I do" to being the church.

- Celebrate key markers in a person's life—birthdays, anniversaries, promotions, a housewarming, the birth of a child. Don't wait for social media to remind you. Keep your own records.

- Find a parent who needs help, especially if you're an empty nester or older single person.

- Go beyond offering apologies. Practice asking for forgiveness when a misunderstanding occurs. Consider the "foes" you discovered in the previous exercise.

- Collect "cultural artifacts" that reflect your group (recipes, poems, paintings, songs, stories, etc.). Have everyone contribute something representative.

5

THE RHYTHM OF COMPASSION

Learning to See Others' Needs
as Merely Different from Your Own

*[Jesus said,] "You will receive power when
the Holy Spirit comes on you."*

ACTS 1:8

WHEN I MET JONATHAN, he had been in Austin just a few months. He was taking ESL classes with my friend Ashley. He fled the violence and hardships of military-ruled Myanmar (also known as Burma) in 2007, walking twenty-one days through the Thai jungle to Malaysia. Seeing how many kids weren't being cared for, he began taking language classes, inviting five children to join him. After eight years, this became an international Christian boarding school with two hundred students and thirty faculty in partnership with graduate students from the University of Malaya. Jonathan had more faith than funding. After receiving permission from the United Nations, he chose Austin, Texas, to reunite with other villagers from the Chin State in Myanmar and to begin a new life with his family.

The school is still going, now run by the United Nations High Council for Refugees.[1]

With Jonathan's help, our small church start-up visited his community in small groups armed with bags of groceries, children's clothing, and a translator, if needed. At each home, we'd begin by saying, "Hi! We wanted to welcome you to Austin. We're so glad you're here! Hospitality is one of the ways we like to express our faith in God. We were wondering: How long have you been here? Have you been able to find work? And is there anything we can pray for?" Before we left, we'd offer our provisions. One lady, Sam, who has now become an amazing seamstress, a skilled sushi chef, and a dear friend, said this was the first time in seven years that any Americans (or Christians) had been in her home. At first, I felt a sense of pride, as if I deserved a pat on the back. But very quickly, I sensed the Holy Spirit gently helping me realize, *I've been in Austin for ten years, and I've never had an immigrant in my home.* At this moment, I knew we were on holy ground. We each had things to offer, and we each had needs.

COMPASSION AS ORDINARY *AND* UNNATURAL

In the New Testament, we learn that Jesus is not asking His followers to perform distant acts of charity. He seeks concrete acts of love: feeding the hungry, welcoming the stranger, providing clothing to the needy, visiting the prisoner (Matthew 25:31-36). Compassion is less of a behavior to adopt and more a part of our design, which is why new life is experienced when we find outlets to care for and support others. In Hebrew, the language of the Old Testament, the word *compassion* in several places translates as "mercy," "tender love," and even "womb."[2] The picture is of birthing. That is a life-giving act. If we apply this to our human experience, *our compassionate actions always give the other person another chance. We can all author life because of our capacity to offer help and hope.*

In other words, in showing compassion, I do not hold past failures against another person. Instead, I offer a fresh start. I choose to view another's current circumstances or challenges not as simply "their problem." It's incredible to think that we *all* have the power to give life by choosing to operate with compassion!

Compassion can be a complicated topic to communicate. We often hear "You're not doing enough," or "God is compassionate, so you should be too" . . . without much explanation of the why or how behind these statements. That's because compassion is learned more through experience than from a sermon. We learn about compassion when we feel its impact. Sometimes we're the ones in need; at other times we're the givers. As compassion becomes a rhythm in our lives, it can keep our hearts sensitive—not just to meet others' needs but also to hear God's voice.

Compassion as a Christian response occurs as we see the image of God in others. A rhythm for resensitizing our hearts creates fertile soil for God to use compassion to shape us more into His image. This is how we experience new life and have a living faith! When we practice compassion, we act as cocreators with God in restoring and repairing a broken world.

The spiritual rhythm of compassion is learning to see others' needs as simply different from our own.

Since charity is typically offered from a place of financial power, it's easy to miss the deepening effects of giving and receiving. Learning to see others' needs as merely different from our own means we start seeing that all of us are needy *and* all of us have something to give *and* everyone has something to learn, even from the most unlikely sources. Approaching the rhythm of compassion this way helps form our hearts in the likeness of Christ. This approach moves compassion from simply adding or adopting behaviors to shaping the posture of our hearts to be changed from the inside out.

Nothing about John the Baptist sounds hospitable, much less compassionate. His sense of fashion was odd, he distanced himself from the mainstream, and his social skills skewed more toward confrontational than comforting. In Luke 3, we find him baptizing people outside the religious establishment of Jerusalem. Yet he drew a diverse crowd of observant Jews, tax collectors, and soldiers. As the religious leaders approached, he promptly greeted them by calling them a bunch of snakes (Luke 3:7). He was angry at the religious leaders because they neglected the needy among them. They were more confident in their heritage than compassionate to those in the margins. He even threatened them, saying, "The ax is already at the root" (Luke 3:9), which meant that, even though they were God's chosen people, their favor with God was in jeopardy because they neglected the poor and vulnerable. The crowd asked, "What should we do then?" John began with "Anyone who has two shirts should share with the one who has none, and anyone who has food should do the same" (Luke 3:10-11).

It's always meaningful to find an affinity with people close by, especially when they're in the same life stage as you. However, the Bible's command to "love your neighbor as yourself" (Mark 12:31) isn't merely about caring for those near you. Chances are, the people living close to you reflect a similar educational background and income level, so their material needs likely won't seem that much different from yours. The challenge of loving our neighbor is that it requires willingness to cross social divides where needs, perspectives, incomes, and education are primarily different from our own. *This* is where the Spirit finds the most fertile soil to shape our hearts as both givers and receivers.

Most Christians I know are happy to help when they see people in need, but because of their lack of proximity to those in need, they don't encounter opportunities often. Few people who have resources and privilege are willing to go beyond the safety and familiarity of their neighborhood to build relationships and identify needs. I find it fascinating that when we cross social barriers, it inevitably reframes our concept of what a person needs and what is enough. It can help recalibrate both our gratitude for what we have and our concern for what others lack.

As noted earlier, our faith community found a unique friendship with a group of immigrants from Myanmar. After more than a year of visiting homes, sharing meals, having fun events, and praying together, I asked my friend Thanla Tan if the groceries and clothes our church was donating were helpful to his Burmese community. He said, "Yes, the community is very thankful. *But* . . . the thing they like most is when you pray with them and for their families." I responded, "Really? They'd rather have our prayers than a meal from us?" He gently replied with a grin, "Pastor . . . meals are good, but prayers are best!"

Let me be clear: Establishing a rhythm of offering both tangible gifts and prayer is needed, as one without the other is lacking. However, to this community of believers who live with little material wealth, prayer was a cherished and compassionate gift. Perhaps it's because through our prayers with and for them, we were showing compassion and solidarity. (There's much more to say about nurturing one's prayer life, but this chapter is more about allowing God to shape our hearts through compassion.) Learning to trust and rely on God through our prayers as well as the prayers of others can feel unnatural, if not uncomfortable.

My prayers have changed over the last few years because of my friendships with people in this Burmese community. I still have many requests for both desires and needs. But my shifted perspective has also helped me not lose faith in the absence of direct answers. Silence from God doesn't feel like not being heard. And prayer isn't just about asking God for things. I find myself asking God *about* things, which has a softening effect on my heart.

Outward expressions of faith, like compassion, can reveal the work of the Holy Spirit. And it should be noted that the Holy Spirit often speaks through other believers. The chance to apprentice is a chance not only to walk in the Spirit but also to sustain the work of the Holy Spirit. While part of following Christ is a calling to act with care and justice, we can do only so much through our own strength. But the result of compassion isn't merely limited to good works. When we understand and align with the Holy Spirit's power, our compassion transforms both giver and receiver. Our task is to be sensitive and responsive to the Spirit's leading and trust God with the results.

Scripture reveals how compassion shows God's heart for the

world. Salvation is not just for our benefit. It should also benefit others. This is what being saved or born again entails—sharing the Good News with others in tangible ways. We often think of salvation as only a spiritual condition (i.e., status: saved). And it is, but it's also much more. The salvation that Jesus brings means that war, addiction, hunger, divorce, resentment, abuse, and other tragedies of this broken world don't have to be the final word.

THE GOD WHO SEES

In Genesis 16, we're introduced to El Roi, The God Who Sees. It's the scene where Hagar, Sarai's servant girl, fled camp after being given to Abram as a wife to bear a child for Sarai. She incurred jealousy and scorn from Sarai and decided that being alone in the wilderness was better than taking more abuse. God met her in her despair and made a promise similar to the one that He made to Abram. Hagar's abuse wasn't what God intended, and He saw her pain! Similarly, God sees our debt, addiction, hypocrisy, tears, and lack of care. He sees our discipline, integrity, compassion, generosity, extra effort, and anonymous contribution. And because He sees, God hears, cares, acts, and grieves with us. So what if we consider the possibility that our emotions are not an end in themselves? What if the things we see and the injustice and inequity we grieve are also what God feels? Much of the way we experience life is through our feelings. Emotions should lead us somewhere, not get us stuck. Since we are created in the image of God, the question is *What do we do with what we see?* Maybe the invitation is to be a part of a solution in the present.

God sees abuse, injustice, hunger, abandonment, and despair. What's more, He cares. God sees . . . genocide, child soldiers, human trafficking, child prostitution, and wars in the Middle East. He sees the Oval Office and home offices, mistakes to be made and careers to be chosen, accidents about to happen and accidents that almost happened, runaways living on their own and prodigals far from home. God sees what we see and then some. He is The God Who Sees.

It's natural to feel overwhelmed by what's wrong in our world. It can cause us to become guarded, to insulate ourselves from being too affected. But what if God plans to have our hearts broken for all the right reasons? We often look around at our lives and this world, wondering, *Where's God?* Or *How could He let that happen?* We feel like God should be more active. Oftentimes, God's general and special revelation in each of us can be seen in what captures (or breaks) our hearts or feels like an injustice. So . . .

> What if a large part of what we feel about greed, scarcity, abuse, wealth, and accomplishment is supposed to help us see what God sees?
>
> What if much of what we feel is more like a road than the destination?
>
> What if the things we see that make us mad or sad are also what God sees? And the disgust we feel is also what God feels?
>
> What if that's how God is operating in this world—in us and through us?

The good news is that we're not without a response of our own in simple, small ways. Philosopher and theologian

Jean-Yves Lacoste describes emotions as the halfway point of understanding and says that how we feel is an indication to look not only for understanding but for God.[3] I think our emotions are supposed to help us experience something God already sees, grieves, and wants to remedy. Ever wonder why some issues resonate deeply with certain people but not with others? There are things I see as a problem, unjust, or unhealthy that others disregard, and vice versa. Often, these are issues God allows us to see and calls us to respond to. Everyone has a calling. Everyone's heart needs to grow. And everyone's life is created to align with the image of a living God. When practiced, compassion helps us discover our calling. Caring for God's creation is a stewardship issue. As we feel loss, injustice, or even anger at the things in our world, God tries to move us to care for the people and address the needs around us.

Herein lies a monumental challenge. Like any feeling, compassion is hard to sustain . . . in our own strength, that is. There's only so much help we can offer, only so much time we have to offer it in, and only so much sadness or anger we can absorb before we want to retreat, grow cynical, or become ambivalent. But this reveals the essential piece of the Christian life: How do we live the Jesus life that we're called to but can't live on our own? We can't—but we're not supposed to. What if a spiritual rhythm of compassion is also a significant gateway to experiencing the Holy Spirit?

RECENTERING AND RECALIBRATING

In between bites of fresh guacamole and Tex-Mex tacos, I listened to Shane,[4] a single, well-spoken, thirty-year-old sales rep.

We've shared many meals, with conversations covering sports, friendship, dating, faith, politics, goals, and ambitions. This conversation sounded familiar as Shane described his lack of motivation, even discipline, for his job. He said, "I can mail it in and still get by." On the side, for fun, Shane had started taking some acting classes. He'd been doing auditions and had even landed a few parts in local productions. Despite the demands on his time, he enjoyed letting out his inner artist. And this wasn't a new experience for Shane. A couple of years earlier, he had booked several consecutive college-football weekends, just like he had in college. However, nothing changed in his lack of motivation. So I shared with him, "You have the good fortune of having a job that gives you a lot of discretionary time and doesn't demand your soul. You've found a creative outlet. And you can still enjoy weekend getaways in pursuit of fun." Then, more gently, I continued, "The thing that might be missing is you giving yourself permission to do something beyond yourself. There's nothing you're doing of consequence for someone else. And yet, I believe we're created to give our lives away even without being repaid."

The apostle Paul, as he grew in faith, was able to view both his success and his suffering in light of what God saw. His accomplishments didn't prevent him from depending on God, nor did his struggles keep him from trusting in God. Paul learned to be "content whatever the circumstances. . . . Whether well fed or hungry, whether living in plenty or in want" (Philippians 4:11-12). A compassionate perspective, in light of the grace of God, is that we are all in need.

Our lives—including our gifts, time, experiences, resources, influence, and health—are not created to be hoarded or stored. Our lives are meant to be shared. Here's the rub, though: Many people desire meaning but are consumed with work and/or leisure. Many long to be benevolent and generous but settle for being self-indulgent. While it's valuable to have personally rewarding outlets, we also need to consider the spiritual practice of not becoming the center of our own lives! The best practice we can adopt (and try to instill in our apprentices) is to develop an outwardly loving discipline. Admittedly, compassion is hard to sustain. As we offer ourselves—and trust God with the results—we practice keeping Christ at the center of our lives. This is the deepening work of the Holy Spirit.

EVIDENCE OF THE HOLY SPIRIT

Many of us grew up with a predictable and controlled view of the Trinity. And for many, the third person of the Trinity feels like the least understood and the least frequently applicable to daily Christian life. Few Christians deny the power of the Holy Spirit, but words often fail to describe the Spirit's functional role adequately. More than being an emotional response to us or a limited manifestation of God, God's Spirit seeks to have an ever-expanding work in the life of every disciple. What's more, only the ongoing work of the Spirit gives us agency to sustain, if not grow in, compassion.

It can be a little tricky trying to understand and recognize the activity of God's Spirit. This is especially true in Western contexts, where citizens cry for empirical evidence or repeatable history while many church traditions cling to creeds and static doctrines. Try as we might, we can't self-help our way to transformation. And no number of good deeds can make us more lovable to God. Simply put, we can't save ourselves. We need the Spirit of God within our lives. We experience the indwelling of God's Spirit as we believe. Jesus also promised His disciples another baptism (Acts 1:5-8). The infilling of the Holy Spirit helps us live the life we're called to live but can't live in our own strength. What signs are evidence that God's Spirit empowers, enables, and orchestrates something beyond us, beyond our human capacity, as we see in the early church? The increasing and infilling work of the Holy Spirit has (at least) a fivefold witness:

1. a greater capacity to love;
2. a greater power for obedience;
3. a greater boldness in our witness;
4. our verbal expression; and
5. the fruit of the Spirit.

Let's look at each one individually.

A Greater Capacity to Love

We all face people who are simply hard to love. Maybe they have different opinions or have done something to hurt us. Perhaps they come from a different culture, display different reactions, or feel like a threat. The Holy Spirit can meet us in our weaknesses and human limitations and help us express compassion, care, grace, patience, and mercy. Growing a relationship with the Holy Spirit means we ask ourselves questions like these: *Do I love God now more than I did a year ago? Do I grieve injustice more? Do I find more beauty in creation and diversity? Am I more patient? Is my heart more sensitized to the Spirit's guidance?* This is the difference between knowing all humans are made in the image of God and being enabled by the Holy Spirit to love our neighbors well (see Luke 23:34).

Adolf Eichmann was the mastermind behind Hitler's genocide of the Jews. Fifteen years after the end of World War II, in 1960, he was finally captured in Argentina and brought to trial. Among the witnesses called to testify against him was a small, haggard man named Yehiel Dinur, who had survived brutal torture in the death camp at Auschwitz. Dinur entered the courtroom; he stared at the man who had presided over the slaughter of millions, including many of Dinur's friends. As the eyes of the victim met those of the mass murderer, the courtroom fell silent. Then, suddenly, Dinur collapsed to the floor, sobbing violently.[5] Was he overcome by hatred as memories surfaced of the stark evil that Eichmann had committed? No. As Dinur explained later, in a 60 Minutes interview with Mike Wallace, what struck him was that Eichmann did not look like an evil monster. He looked like an ordinary person. Just like anyone else. "I was afraid about myself," Dinur said. "I saw that I am capable to do this. I am . . . exactly like he." In a remarkable conclusion, Wallace said: "Eichmann is in all of us."[6] In other words, we're all equally flawed. At the same time, however, we all are unconditionally loved by God. It's not natural to love this way. But the Holy Spirit enables us to love even the most unlovable.

When he wrote his letter to the believers in Ephesus, Paul was in jail for making salvation available to non-Jews.

Nevertheless, he didn't seem angry, maybe because Paul didn't see himself as any better than his accusers. He didn't pray for his circumstances to be better or easier. Instead, Paul prayed for the Ephesians: "I pray that you, being rooted and established in love, may have power . . . to grasp how wide and long and high and deep is the love of Christ" (Ephesians 3:17-18). We shouldn't be defined by wealth, mistakes, luck, regret, broken relationships, class, or culture. We emerge with a new identity as we understand who we are in light of who God is. We are hidden in Christ, not buried by circumstances. As we seek to make amends or give up control, it begins with experiencing how deep and wide God's love is and how long and high it is. That's a change from the inside out.

The idea that we're supposed to love our neighbor as ourselves (Matthew 22:39) is well known and accepted. And depending on how much you enjoy the people who live near you, this might not be challenging for you. However, the idea of being "in community" with people is, at least to some extent, different. When the Bible challenges us to love our neighbor, it's an invitation to cross social divides and love people who don't look or act or think like us. Practicing compassion starts with spending time with people whose needs differ from our own. It often requires a willingness to cross social divides simply because, in the end, we need each other.

Lois Tverberg, cofounder of En-Gedi Resource Center and researcher of first-century Judaism, shares helpful insight on how ancient rabbis interpreted the commandment to love our neighbors (and implications for twenty-first-century Christians):

The commonly understood interpretation is that we should love others with the same measure that we love ourselves, which is certainly very true! But the [ancient] rabbis also saw that the Hebrew of that verse can also be read as, 'Love your neighbor *who is like yourself.*' While either interpretation is valid, [the rabbis'] emphasis was less on comparing love of ourselves with love for others, and more on comparing *other people* to ourselves, and then loving them because they are like us in our own frailties. . . . When we realize that we are guilty of the same sins that others are, we see that we shouldn't bear grudges against them, but forgive and love them instead.[7]

A Greater Power for Obedience

When we depend on sheer willpower or a charitable mood, compassionate obedience is difficult, if not impossible, to sustain. But where God calls, God provides. God calls each of us into obedience, not as a burden or obligation but out of love. God also knows our needs. The Holy Spirit is often evidence of God's presence to empower us to turn from temptation, help without being asked, give without recognition, or obey even when our strength and courage are lacking (see Acts 3:1-10; 7:51-60).

Over time, we realize that activities, words, and thoughts that once felt permissible now feel increasingly unbeneficial. The Holy Spirit has a way of courting us into obedience as intimacy with Him changes our desires. To what extent do you experience a "check" in your spirit, a moment of pause or hesitation? Have you ever felt compelled to turn toward or away from an idea, attitude, person, or behavior? It's these moments that, over time, become an increasingly familiar activity of God's Spirit, drawing us closer to God's likeness.

Sam, at sixty-eight, had been a pastor, professor, and missionary, but due to his wife's dementia, he was now providing her full-time care. He still loved making time for tired pastors with big worries, so we met over breakfast. We were talking about prayer, about my frustration with not hearing from God. In response, Sam told me a story. He had just finished bathing his wife, putting her diaper on, and getting her dressed when he got a whiff of a foul smell. Realizing she had just messed up her pants, he took her clothes back off to clean her up. As she stood there, she went again, right on the bathroom floor. With a tear rolling down his cheek, the emotion still fresh, he told me he turned to God angrily and said, *I've had it! I can't take it! Can You hear me?!?* I started to offer my condolences. "Sam, I'm so sorry . . ." But he interrupted me, explaining, "David, God continues asking us the same question: 'Can *you* hear *Me*?'" Sam's powerful story reminded me how God speaks in suffering as much as in prosperity. The struggle isn't a punishment from God but an invitation to trust Him, express our needs, and feel that He is near.

The Holy Spirit can provide greater power for obedience, for instance, to keep our vows in marriage and faith. It can often feel both hard and good. But this is what intimacy looks like, even when life unravels. Sometimes compassion feels like the most natural response. Other times, it feels like a bothersome effort. Yet compassionate obedience, on any level, allows the Holy Spirit room to care for others while also recentering our lives in Christ.

A Greater Boldness in Our Witness

Have you ever had a conversation with someone in a difficult spot? You didn't prepare, and you couldn't recreate the conversation if you tried. What's more, you need help to recall precisely what you said. All you know is that you shared meaningful insight, counsel, or comfort. Other times, we're compelled to share our personal experiences—a question gets asked, an observation is made, or an idea is shared. And before we talk ourselves out of it, a conversation has often begun, and the Spirit guides us. The compulsion to bear witness to Christ is often prompted by the work of the Spirit (Acts 1:8; 4:1-22, 31; 2 Corinthians 4:13-15).

Compassion invites us to step outside the bubble of our largely homogenous communities so that our hearts, minds, and faith may be resensitized. Often, when we do cross social barriers, we feel more alive and grateful. The Holy Spirit creates an inward richness that transcends our financial net worth. It weaves together our life experiences like a divine tapestry. God's Spirit gives us eyes to see needs different from our own. It's this inner prompting that allows us to grow in boldness.

In *The Prophetic Imagination*, Walter Brueggemann writes, "Compassion constitutes a radical form of criticism, for it announces that the hurt is to be taken seriously, that the hurt is not to be accepted as normal and natural but is an abnormal and unacceptable condition for humanness. . . . The compassion of

Jesus is to be understood not simply as a personal emotional reaction but as a public criticism in which he dares to act upon his concern against the entire numbness of his social context."[8] A significant part of the deepening work of God's Spirit is that we respond to our God-prompted convictions in increasing measure over time. Doing so can move us to advocacy, relief work, and sacrificial choices. It might even mean becoming part of the answer to our own prayer requests.

Our Verbal Expression

One of the initial demonstrations of the Holy Spirit within the early church was what came out of the believers' mouths. In the book of Acts, when the Holy Spirit came upon them, they "spoke the word of God boldly" (Acts 4:31), spoke a word of knowledge, and spoke in tongues and prophesied (Acts 2:4; 5:1-11; 19:6). Additionally, Stephen's accusers "could not stand up against the wisdom the Spirit gave him as he spoke" (Acts 6:10), and Gentiles were "speaking in tongues and praising God" (Acts 10:46; also see Romans 2:28-29). Verbal expression seems to be consistently associated with the manifestation and ongoing activity of the Holy Spirit.

If we learn anything from Pentecost, we learn that the Holy Spirit transcends tradition, culture, ethnicity, and religion: the Galilean disciples were "declaring the wonders of God in [foreign languages]" (Acts 2:11). Pentecost is thought of as the day the church began. The problem is that when we hear the word *church*, we picture a building with a worship service lined with pews and perhaps a stage that suggests something like performance art. The day the church began was more than a spectacle to be observed by the masses. It was the day that each believer heard "in [their] own languages" (Acts 2:11, NLT). The Holy Spirit speaks in the most personal, nuanced way, not only through various tongues but also in understandable vernacular. Verbal expression is what makes the revelation of God accessible to others. It's an essential part of the Christian witness, yet our words are also a significant way we reflect God's character and nature. To what extent do your words—which express your humor, intellect, biases, resentments, insecurities, and hopes—reflect God as the pioneer and perfecter of faith (see Hebrews 12:2)?

We don't often think of our speech as an act of faith, but do we trust God with our reputation and validation, or do we feel like we always need to get the last word? Does giving an apology feel like losing? The point is this: Language matters. Do we think we need words to justify ourselves, or can God as our witness be our defense? The ways we communicate should change as our faith grows.

Our language can bear just as much fruit as our deeds. It might take some reorientating, but try to imagine your speech as a means of expressing faith in God and compassion to others. It's always a powerful testimony when words are gracious, insightful, comforting, truthful, encouraging, and wise. This is how the Holy Spirit is manifest in our conversations as well as our worship. Conversely, curses, accusations, criticism, gossip, or innuendos only reveal what's in the heart. They're neither a helpful witness nor, more importantly, evidence that the holiness of God's Spirit is active in one's heart.

This is where small-batch disciplemaking plays such a vital

role. When someone knows us well, they are able to see our blind spots and hear something in our voice that we are often unaware of. "You know when you said that, this is how it comes across." We need to let the Spirit guide our words instead of automatically sharing unfiltered comments. Left up to my natural self, I might share more sarcasm and cynicism. Without the infilling work of the Holy Spirit, I'm prone to articulate fear more than hope, despair more than gratitude, anger more than grace. Part of how the Spirit works is through convicting our hearts and through the counsel of discipling leaders who know us well and have our development in mind.

The Fruit of the Spirit

The fruit described in Galatians 5:22-23 is not to be addressed one at a time. This "fruit" of love, joy, peace, forbearance (patience), kindness, goodness, faithfulness, gentleness, and self-control is evidence of the Spirit dwelling inside us. This fruit is often what is seen in unexpected and challenging moments. It's what comes out in the face of stress, tragedy, opposition, crisis, or uncertainty. As we work to align our hearts with God, the Spirit helps us find a kind of harmonic resonance. A tuning fork is used to tune musical instruments. When struck against a surface, it begins vibrating, resonating at a particular pitch that is a pure tone. Spiritually, harmonic resonance occurs when our spirit becomes increasingly attuned to God's Spirit. It's a growing awareness of God's presence in daily living as we align ourselves with God's Holy Spirit. This kind of harmony is experienced (by us and others) as our lives produce fruit.

From the beginning, God planned to bless and provide for us and use us to bless and provide for others. Jewish teachers throughout history have suggested that failing to offer provisions for the poor is robbing the poor.[9] The Bible is about identifying the vulnerable and needy because we're not that different from them. It teaches us to reflect on God and live in the Kingdom of heaven here and now. Central to our understanding of what it means to follow Jesus is making accommodations for the needs among us, although the Bible doesn't insist that we take vows of poverty. Compassion means recognizing a person's needs that are merely different from one's own—and helping meet them. We all have needs and we all have resources. As we seek a greater infilling of the Holy Spirit, our lives bear the fruit of God's saving work in us and through us.

DISCUSSION QUESTIONS

1. Do you think someone can be changed by the Holy Spirit and still struggle, even stumble, with an old pattern? Does stumbling negate the change?

2. Since compassion doesn't always come naturally or feel comfortable, how can we sustain this rhythm . . . or even become *more* compassionate?

3. Many people have a vague understanding of the Holy Spirit. People are often left to relate to the Trinity as Father, Son, and Holy Scriptures because the Bible might feel more accessible to them than the Holy Spirit. There's not enough explanation or

understanding of how God's Spirit operates today, in the here and now. Based on this chapter, how would you describe the person and work of the Holy Spirit to a seven-year-old?

4. How does the perspective that our emotions can reveal God's heart and our calling change how you relate to God?

5. In what areas does this perspective shed light on your sense of calling to a cause or particular concern?

Finding Your Rhythm

Sustaining the Work of Compassion
and Cultivating the Infilling of the Holy Spirit

A SIGNIFICANT APPRENTICING experience involves practicing compassion, even if it's not reciprocated. A changed
life is evident when we serve others as an ongoing part of our
daily lives. But this is where we realize how limited we are
in sustaining compassion as a regular practice. Compassion
only sometimes means doing a series of service projects
outside our everyday activities. Instead, God intends for us
to discover a rhythm of compassion
as a part of our ordinary lives.
Being transformed by compassion requires the activity of the
Holy Spirit to do for us what we
can't sustain on our own.

THE TRANSFORMING POWER OF THE SPIRIT

What do you think is the function or role of the Spirit? In 1 John 2:1, John writes, "My dear children, I write this to you so that you will not sin. But if anybody does sin, we have an advocate with the Father—Jesus Christ, the Righteous One." The word translated *advocate* here is from the Greek word *paraklētos*. Let's break it down to its parts. *Para*, in this case, means "to the side of."[10] We can see this usage carried over to our words parallel and paramedic. The second part, *klētos*, comes from the verb *kaleō*, which means "to call out," or "to invite."[11] Put the two together, and we begin to understand that the role of the Holy Spirit is as one who comes to the side of and speaks for. With the Holy Spirit dwelling in us, compassion is a tangible way to come alongside and meet others' needs. When Jesus promises the Holy Spirit in John 14, we find further evidence of the Spirit's empowering work:

> "If you love me, keep my commands. And I will ask the Father, and he will give you another advocate to help you and be with you forever—the Spirit of truth. The world cannot accept him, because it neither sees him nor knows him. But you know him, for he lives with you and will be in you. I will not leave you as orphans; I will come to you. Before long, the world will not see me anymore, but you will see me. Because I live, you also will live. . . .
>
> "All this I have spoken while still with you. But the Advocate, the Holy Spirit, whom the Father will send in my name, will teach you all things and will remind you of everything I have said to you. Peace I leave with

you; my peace I give you. I do not give to you as the
world gives. Do not let your hearts be troubled and
do not be afraid."

JOHN 14:15-19, 25-27

1. Based on these passages highlighting Jesus' physical
   departure, what does the Holy Spirit give us that we
   can't do or get on our own?

2. What changed about God's work when Jesus ascended?

The apostle Paul also explains the Holy Spirit's role. In his
epistle to the believers in Rome, he says:

In the same way, the Spirit helps us in our weakness.
We do not know what we ought to pray for, but the
Spirit himself intercedes for us through wordless
groans. And he who searches our hearts knows the
mind of the Spirit, because the Spirit intercedes for
God's people in accordance with the will of God.

ROMANS 8:26-27

A COMPASSION AUDIT
Reread this quote from Walter Brueggemann and answer the questions below.

> Compassion constitutes a radical form of criticism, for it announces that the hurt is to be taken seriously, that the hurt is not to be accepted as normal and natural but is an abnormal and unacceptable condition for humanness. . . . The compassion of Jesus is to be understood not simply as a personal emotional reaction but as a public criticism in which he dares to act upon his concern against the entire numbness of his social context.

3. Do you know any Christians, either personally or at a distance, who embody the kind of radical compassion described in this quote?

4. It's interesting to think of compassion as public criticism. How could compassion be expressed within your regular social context?

5. Compassion can feel inconvenient or like an interruption. It also can make us feel vulnerable. Why is compassion necessary for our own sake?

6. In what ways have your reactions to experiencing stress, fear, or loss changed over time as you've grown spiritually? How have your coping mechanisms changed?

A PASSION AUDIT

A significant aspect of uncovering our calling from God is understanding what moves our hearts. Compassion is one way God moves us to action. People differ in their concerns and awareness of needs, but we all need to learn how God has prepared us to respond when something stirs our compassion. God often reveals a sense of calling and mission rooted in what motivates us internally and/or passionately. **Answer the questions below, and mark the categories that you feel passionate about.**

7. What are you passionate about? What excites you about helping others? Are there any nonprofits or underserved people groups you currently work with?

8. What is your holy discontent, the need you feel compelled to meet or the cause you are drawn to address? What issue grieves or saddens you? What problem do you see that makes you think, *That's not fair!*, *That's not right!*, or *Someone should do something about that!*?

Below is an incomplete list of categories to help with your passion audit. Each represents a population or aspect of society with unique needs. Potential volunteer opportunities corresponding to these unique needs are identified in parentheses. Mark which categories resonate with you, and feel free to add your own.

_____ children and youth (e.g., teach Sunday school; become a Big Brother or Big Sister mentor; volunteer for an organization serving children who have been abused, trafficked, or placed in foster care)

_____ elderly (e.g., read to people in hospice care; play games with residents at an assisted-living facility; conduct home visits)

_____ poverty and food insecurity (e.g., become a volunteer at a food pantry or soup kitchen; assist at a homeless shelter or a job-placement organization)

_____ immigrants and refugees (e.g., teach ESL [English as a Second Language]; provide transportation, childcare, or cultural orientation; train in job development or money management)

_____ disabled (e.g., assist with speech therapy; volunteer with social, recreational, or educational tutoring programs)

_____ education (e.g., volunteer with an organization reducing illiteracy; become a tutor to children of migrant workers; read with children who are below reading level for their grade)

_____ environment (e.g., educate people on climate change; advocate for renewable energy and repurposing goods; start a recycling program at a location that doesn't have one)

_____ teen parents (e.g., provide mentoring; schedule play dates or book/diaper drives; become a wellness advisor)

_____ other: _____

_____

_____

Use the self-knowledge and ideas you've gleaned from this passion audit as a springboard for turning your compassion into action.

9. Whether you're a disciplemaker or an apprentice (or both!), what opportunities do you have to practice compassion together, perhaps regularly? Is someone you know already working with a particular need that others could help them with?

6

THE RHYTHM OF GENEROSITY

Seeing God as the Source . . . and Surrendering to Him

[Jesus said,] "I am the vine; you are the branches."

JOHN 15:5

STARLA IS A GIFTED PROFESSIONAL ARTIST who layers much texture and detail into her paintings.[1] When she built a new studio and invited me to visit, I jumped at the opportunity. It was a bright, inspiring space, and I got to see many of her original pieces. She began talking about training an eye to see beyond the surface. "You have to see with your imagination and look beyond what is on the surface. . . . There's always more than what meets the eye," Starla explained. If you're familiar with Starla's art, you can understand her description of how this process works. She added:

> When we lose our capacity to have childlike faith
> and wonder about the world, we get tunnel vision.

Our intellect, reasoning, and fact collecting dull our imaginations. As grown-ups, we think everything should have an explanation and that there is no such thing as the supernatural and unexplainable. As an artist, it's my job to keep a childlike imagination and to see. To be able to see correctly, you have to get on your knees and humbly ask our Lord to give you eyes that can see.

Listening to Starla, I was reminded of the apostle Paul's words to the believers in Ephesus: "I pray that the eyes of your heart may be enlightened in order that you may know the hope to which he has called you, the riches of his glorious inheritance in his holy people, and his incomparably great power for us who believe" (Ephesians 1:18-19).

Like Starla, Paul implies there's another way to see—in layers. In other words, we need to train our eyes to see beyond the surface. Paul's prayer is not about physical eyes but rather about spiritual eyes, about a more profound way of seeing needs, opportunities, and our resources differently in light of our Christian identity. As we practice a rhythm of generosity, we are invited to see in a new way with the backdrop of God as the Source.

When it comes to our wealth, success, talent, abilities, education, and relationships, it's easy to think that we earned it because we worked hard. But what if you could help someone see that all life is a gift and that everything one has—health, friends, influence, literacy, health care, a full pantry, clean drinking water—is part of God's gracious provision? The best way to learn to practice generosity is when someone close to you helps you see how much you already have and challenges you to invest your life as a sacred trust. Generosity requires coaching. We need reminders to interrupt feelings of scarcity or to avoid development of callouses that suggest others' needs are someone else's problem. We need mirrors to reflect how much we do have. And we need someone we're in proximity with and whom we can depend on to help us demonstrate, invite, and even celebrate this sacred trust. Ultimately—and this requires a fresh perspective—God is the Source of our lives. He invites us to be trustees of the resources He has given us so that we might increasingly give our lives away.

Growing in generosity means becoming more aware of the needs, opportunities, and resources already present in our lives. In other words, we don't need to wait to have more time, money, talent, or recognition to embody the generous nature of God.

A SACRED TRUST

Have you ever thought about the difference between a steward and a trustee? In general, when we talk about finances in the church, we use the language of stewardship. However, stewardship can be a limited metaphor to talk about leveraging resources. One of its definitions implies "I'm a good manager of what's mine." A trustee, on the other hand, is always someone charged with caring for someone else's estate. If we extend the metaphor to our spiritual lives, a steward might approach giving from a perspective of "what's mine," while a trustee would see themselves as managing *God's* estate. Obviously, both are good. Neither would be considered "the right way." But perhaps framing our giving from a trustee perspective might help us hold our possessions and resources more loosely in light of God's grace. So as we grow as disciples on mission, the critical question isn't *How much should I give back to God?* He already owns the estate. Rather, we need to ask, *How much should I keep for myself if it's all God's?*[2] In a sense, we're all spiritually trust fund babies![3] We've all been entrusted with some level of health, wealth, influence, experience, education, intellect, and giftedness that is God's gracious extension of Himself.

The rhythm of generosity offers a renewed way to understand our role as spiritual trustees. As we learn to see God as the Source of our lives, we see that all life is a gift. So everything we've been given (or even worked for) . . . it's all a gift. Realizing that all we have is a gift—a sacred trust—we can learn to hold all these things with open hands. Paul also wrote this to Ephesus's young, multicultural church:

> God saved you by his grace when you believed. And you can't take credit for this; it is a gift from God. Salvation is not a reward for the good things we have done, so none of us can boast about it. For we are God's masterpiece. He has created us anew in Christ Jesus, so we can do the good things he planned for us long ago.
>
> EPHESIANS 2:8-10, NLT

Ephesus was renowned for the temple of the goddess Artemis. Her temple was one of the Seven Wonders of the Ancient World, and the city was full of artisans and tradesmen whose income came from artwork depicting Artemis. In Ephesians, Paul surprises his Ephesian audience with his description of grace. Rather than people making art out of God, Paul describes a God who makes art out of people! *Grace is about a God who comes to us, not about us striving toward Him.* We're saved *by* grace *for* good works. And growing in faith should produce something in us. Most notably, love and good works! God seeks to shape each of us into a masterpiece—to create beauty out of our circumstances as we draw near, love outwardly, and trust that He sees the whole canvas. In short, God is irrationally generous when it comes to creation and our humanity. His heart is unmistakably gracious, which for us—as God's image bearers—informs our Christian calling and identity.

You're likely familiar with the concept of karma, the popular idea that if you log enough good, kind, or selfless acts, it will tip some cosmic scale in your favor, but if you're a jerk, it's poetic justice when something bad happens to you. The belief that some force in the universe acts as the great equalizer is compelling to some people, but it's not how God operates. Grace doesn't start or end with the good outweighing the bad. When we consider the enormity of God's grace, we might feel bad about our own paltry efforts. But we shouldn't! God created us in His image to "do the good things he planned for us long ago," as Paul told the Ephesians. God offers us His grace *and* wants us to be His ambassadors (2 Corinthians 5:20).

GOD AS THE SOURCE

I wouldn't be the first person to suggest that money is a better servant than master. Maybe it's helpful, then, to think of generosity as a tuning fork. When handled humbly as an instrument of God, it creates a kind of "harmonic" with the image of God within each of us. As we align our lives in Christ with needs and opportunities around us, our lives become increasingly "in tune" with God. Here's one example of how we can get "in tune" with God's mission.

When I met Ken, he lived in San Francisco with his wife and three children on a very modest income in a costly city. He offered this information willingly, adding that he simply believed God was the Source. He'd been working for an international clothing company, often traveling to manufacturing plants in developing countries, where the conditions were poor and the pay was worse. He was young and new in the business, so he didn't feel he could effect change. At the same time, he sensed a sort of calling to ministry. After a period of discernment with his wife, they answered that call, and he accepted a youth pastor position at a large church in Florida.

Despite successfully working with several hundred high school students and dozens of volunteer leaders, Kenny soon realized he had removed himself from the type of ministry that God was calling him to, ministry in a business setting! He ended up back in San Francisco, where he started a hardwood-floor refinishing business. The city is full of old homes with hardwood floors. Kenny found many people in need of his services. He told me:

These people invite me into their homes. To me, they're not dollar signs. They're people I'm simply invited to bless. We talk about flooring needs, but it often leads to personal family-life stuff. I feel like I get to bless my customers and simply trust God to meet my needs. What's more, I can hire guys coming through recovery programs and incarceration. It's tough for those guys to find good work and not fall back. So I use employment as a chance to disciple these young men in character, family, and trusting in God as their Source.

Fast-forward fifteen years to when my teenage son was working at a local foodie ice-cream shop. His employers didn't even pay minimum wage, but they assured him the tips would be amazing. Except they weren't. With unique flavors like Cilantro Lime, Rosemary-Thyme-Lavender, and Texas Sheet Cake, you can guess that your average customer liked to sample three, four, or even five different flavors. This is where my son quickly developed a profile of the people who don't tip. But when he told me this, I remembered what Ken said about trusting God as the Source. I explained, "Son, anyone coming for ice cream is in a good mood. It's an indulgent, comforting break, usually with family or a friend. Don't see customers as dollar signs. Just see them as people you can bless. If they want to try a couple of flavors, recommend one you like. Chat and celebrate this moment with them. But don't worry about their tip. Trust God to meet your needs, and learn to see yourself as God's instrument with a scoop." Bjorn not only learned to see God's provision beyond his work ethic but also became a generous giver! This is the power of generosity when we see God as the Source: We trust God to meet our needs as we align with His redeeming plans. I find it interesting that the Hebrew word for *righteousness* (*tzedakah*) also translates as *charity*. When we offer our gifts to meet needs, we need to keep in mind that "His righteousness endures forever" (2 Corinthians 9:9, NASB).

DEFINING THE TERMS

Giving and generosity are often used interchangeably but are unique concepts. Let's clarify the terms to understand what they mean.

Giving is the act of releasing something of value in one's possession. Our resources, in whatever form they take, are intended to be for the benefit of others. Understanding this concept comes only when we see all that we have as a gift.

Generosity is a willingness to share with others, which often involves personal sacrifice. The point is not to rob us of anything we worked hard to earn. We hope to be conformed to the image of a generous God who longs to repair and restore a broken world.

A spiritual trustee sees all that they have as a sacred trust for which they will have to give an account. In this plan, we're trying to leverage the resources we've been entrusted with by God. Managing our stuff this way means we have a plan for tithing and not merely "tipping." Second Corinthians 8–9 represents one of the best sections of Scripture on giving and generosity. Early Christians adopted a practice that reflected God's heart. A closer look at the verses reveals unique but transformational ways to align with God's heart. It might be helpful to read the entire two chapters and then discuss them aloud. We can make several observations about giving, generosity, and stewardship from this passage. As you read, look to answer questions like *Whom should we be generous toward?*, *When should we be generous?*, and *How does generosity work?*

In the midst of a very severe trial, their overflowing joy and their extreme poverty welled up in rich generosity. (8:2)	Apparently, generosity is unrelated to income and wealth.
I testify that they gave as much as they were able, and even beyond their ability. (8:3)	Generosity is encouraged but isn't forced.
They gave themselves first of all to the Lord, and then by the will of God also to us. (8:5)	According to this, there's a priority in stewarding resources, and generosity should always be focused on the Lord first.
I am not commanding you, but I want to test the sincerity of your love. (8:8)	When one gives without obligation, generosity is tangible evidence of one's love for God.
At the present time your plenty will supply what they need, so that in turn their plenty will supply what you need. . . . "The one who gathered much did not have too much, and the one who gathered little did not have too little." (8:14-15)	And here's where we learn how generous people— regardless of their net worth—meet needs. It's less about the government or the church and more about God's people responding to need and opportunity.

Each of you should give what you have decided in your heart to give, not reluctantly or under compulsion, for God loves a cheerful giver. (9:7)

True generosity is expressed with a sense of joy and hope. What's more, generosity is personal, between God and us. When it's done in response to God's grace and the Spirit's leading, human recognition or acknowledgment doesn't matter.

Now he who supplies the seed to the sower and bread for food will also supply and increase your store of seed and will enlarge the harvest of your righteousness. You will be enriched in every way so that you can be generous. (9:10-11)

God provides—perhaps even entrusts—blessings and resources for us to practice generosity with.

You will be enriched in every way so that you can be generous on every occasion, and through us your generosity will result in thanksgiving to God.

This service that you perform is not only supplying the needs of the Lord's people but is also overflowing in many expressions of thanks to God. Because of the service by which you have proved yourselves, others will praise God for the obedience that accompanies your confession of the gospel of Christ, and for your generosity. (9:11-13)

If we believe God is generous and gracious, then generosity can move others closer to Him. Being enriched means finding our worth and identity in Christ, not in our status or wealth.

GIVING TO SAVE OURSELVES

In August 2016, Jeni Stepien married Paul Maenner in Swissvale, Pennsylvania. It was more than a perfect wedding day, not because things went off without a hitch but because of who was present. It was ten years after a mugger had killed Jeni's father. Michael Stepien's organs were donated, and the recipient of his heart was a man by the name of Arthur Thomas. For this special occasion, Arthur "Tom" Thomas made the journey from New Jersey to walk Jeni down the aisle. Tom had exchanged letters with Jeni's family over the years. It seemed only fitting to represent Jeni's dad, not only in spirit but also with a significant piece of his physical being. Tom said he had been on death's door until he received Michael's heart. At the wedding, he was filled with emotion. "What greater honor could a person have than walking the daughter of the man who's given his heart to him?" he asked.[4]

If you give your heart, you get His! God is a generous God. It's a natural tendency to think that our effort earns us what we have. But when we can see that everything is rooted in God's provision, we understand that we're not created for self-preservation. God wants us to share in His generous nature. In other words, as you give God your heart—that is, the thing you hold most dear—you also get His heart in increasing ways!

Many of us have given our hearts to Jesus but still long to feel more connected to God. We are more connected than we often realize. The verses I find most troublesome in Scripture are not the ones I disagree with but the ones I struggle to experience. We all encounter times when we lack confidence in what we should do, try, start, create, and risk. In John 15, we learn that Jesus wants His disciples to feel more connected to God and confident in their relationship with Him. He says:

> "I am the true vine, and my Father is the gardener.
> He cuts off every branch in me that bears no fruit,
> while every branch that does bear fruit he prunes so
> that it will be even more fruitful. You are already clean
> because of the word I have spoken to you. Remain in
> me, as I also remain in you. No branch can bear fruit
> by itself; it must remain in the vine. Neither can you
> bear fruit unless you remain in me.
>
> "I am the vine; you are the branches. If you remain
> in me and I in you, you will bear much fruit; apart
> from me you can do nothing. If you do not remain
> in me, you are like a branch that is thrown away and
> withers; such branches are picked up, thrown into the
> fire and burned. If you remain in me and my words
> remain in you, ask whatever you wish, and it will be
> done for you. This is to my Father's glory, that you bear
> much fruit, showing yourselves to be my disciples."
>
> JOHN 15:1-8

Jesus uses a familiar image of the vine, a symbol of Israel itself, in this metaphor. In fact, Herod's temple had a golden vine hanging above the entrance.[5] (This national symbolism would be like stars and stripes for Americans.) After the Last Supper, Jesus said, "I am the true vine, and my Father is the gardener. . . . You are the branches." Think about that for a moment: You are a branch of Jesus! Your identity is rooted in

Him. But what are branches supposed to do? Let's make a few simple observations about reflecting God's generous heart when we're connected to the Vine, our Source:

- *Growth is assumed.* Every living organism grows. The same is true of faith that is alive. The question is always *In which direction are we growing?* Branches on a vine can be left to grow any which way, or they can be trained into order with some effort (i.e., on a trellis or an archway). We, too, can grow more unforgiving, defensive, cynical, and excessive. Or we can develop as more compassionate, generous, gracious, and disciplined through our connection to Jesus, the Vine.

- *Branches bear fruit.* Vines were short and stocky and were cut back for three years before they were allowed to produce. But when they did, it was usually a bumper crop.[6] Perhaps Jesus had the Temple in mind when He said to His disciples, "You have been chosen to bear much fruit" (John 15:16, PAR). Outside Jerusalem, as He says this, is Hinnom Valley with the ever-burning fires of the city dump, a symbol of judgment and sin. The name *Gehenna*, a Greek rendering of *Hinnom Valley*, became a name for hell.[7] As vines are pruned, they need to be burned. Jesus is saying, "If your life is not producing fruit, allow Me to prune you. Let Me cut off that part of your life."

  The fruit is simply multiplying the life of Jesus in you into the life of another. It's how we steward our influence and resources daily to reflect the nature of God. Jesus says to surrender to the pruning.

- *All branches require pruning.* If the branch is fruitful, Jesus goes on to say, it also needs to be pruned. It's the same solution for the branch that bears fruit as it is for the branch that bears no fruit: cut it off. But it's for a different reason! The branch that bears no fruit is cut off so that another one can grow that might be productive. In other words, there's always another chance. But for the branch that *does* bear fruit—where we steward the blessings of God to affect others—it should happen again. Jesus says, "Every branch that does bear fruit he [the Father] prunes *so that* it will be even more fruitful" (emphasis added).

What keeps us from bearing fruit? Not stewarding our blessings for others' benefit. Notice the connection between the love of Jesus and the fruit He wants to see in your life. To bear fruit, we begin with the love of Jesus, which grows a small branch big enough so it can reach others. Generosity, in all aspects of life, is a critical way we bear fruit. John wrote in 1 John 4:18, "There is no fear in love. But perfect love drives out fear." In other words, fear—including fear that the past will affect your future standing before God or that you aren't fully equipped to bear fruit—can prevent us from bearing fruit. But if we abide in God's love, then something happens to our hearts. Our fears are drawn away. Perfect love casts out fear. And fear needs to be cast out.

EXPERIMENTING WITH TRUST

I remember hearing Travis describe his struggle with giving. This guy was gifted enough to be a Division I athlete in two sports! He came from a close, loving family who were all followers of Christ. And they had significant financial resources. During college, Travis was active in volunteering with youth and would testify to God showing up and impacting lives. He'd witnessed God's faithfulness in countless ways. Now, a couple of years removed from college life, he was struggling with biblical stewardship. He was attending a large church, which probably wasn't in any financial need. He was part of a small group of peers but wasn't entirely committed. We talked about how God is the Source of everything. It was clear Travis understood God's abundant provision.

I was surprised when I asked him about tithing.

"Well, I support a couple of buddies I knew in college who are doing ministry," he said.

"Great!" I replied. "That's important and also probably feels good to invest in guys you have a relationship with." I explained that God invites us to participate in both tithes and offerings. A tithe is a systematic way we give based on the firstfruits of our earnings. And since God is always inviting us to take the next steps and be open to His leading, we're also invited to give offerings. An offering is that portion above and beyond our regular giving.

"I know," Travis said, "and I don't disagree with that."

So I pushed a little: "If you say that God is faithful, provides for you, and has blessed you . . . what keeps you from giving from your firstfruits each month?"

With admirable honesty, he replied, "I guess it's because I just have a hard time trusting God that there will be enough at the end of the month."

The apostle Paul writes in 1 Corinthians 4:7, "What do you have that you did not receive?" So then, money (regardless of how much we have) will be a servant or our master. It's tempting to say (or believe in our hearts) that we earned it or somehow deserve it, but herein lies the critical point—and how the Spirit can shape us from within:

> We don't necessarily extend generosity to save others. To be sure, we can make a difference out of our own means. But as disciples and disciplemakers, we extend generosity because it saves us from thinking that we deserve what God has given us.

Even when we trust God to meet our needs, there's a subtle temptation to think we deserve what we have. It's common to think that what we've earned through hard work is ours. We've already seen how God is the true Source of our capacity to earn, work, and thrive. The problem with thinking we are somehow entitled is that it can desensitize us to people who struggle. In his book *Let Your Life Speak*, Parker Palmer wrestles with this common reluctance to be generous. He quotes from a speech by Dorothy Day, cofounder of the Catholic Worker movement, saying, "Do not give to the poor expecting to get their gratitude so that you can feel good about yourself. If you do, your giving will be thin and short-lived, and that is not what the poor need; it will only impoverish them further. Give only if you have something you must give; give only if you are someone for whom giving is its own reward."[8]

In Luke 12:16-21, Jesus tells one of the most offensive, shocking parables. The story describes a rich fool who has more than he needs after harvesting a bumper crop. The man asks himself, *What shall I do with my excess?* This man decides he will build bigger barns to store his surplus; that way he can relax and retire. Instead of sharing from his bounty, he wants to hoard and store. This is one of the only places where Jesus says an act deserves death: "'But God said to him, "You fool! This very night your life will be demanded from you." . . . This is how it will be with whoever stores up things for themselves but is not rich toward God'" (Luke 12:20-21). Much of Jesus' teaching is about grace, acceptance, and mercy, but in this parable, we see God judging the rich fool for his selfishness.

It can be tempting to think that others have more, so *they* should be giving, or that we earned what we have; therefore, we deserve it. But as Christ followers, we are called to give to others and trust God to provide for us. And remember, Jesus doesn't speak favorably about this man's fate. Jesus doesn't indicate any room for "spiritual arrival" or "retirement" in the Kingdom of God.

A rhythm of generosity involves learning to match our strengths with another's weaknesses, our highs with another's lows, and our resources with another's needs. The invitation isn't necessarily to stop every time you see a person looking for a handout. Nor is the answer to divest yourself of your time, energy, and finances for every good cause. However, there is a stewardship opportunity because there is a connection. It's important to discern why this need or opportunity has your attention.

So where do we start? We learn to give without waiting until we have more (time, money, gifts, or experience). The way we learn to give is to leverage what we have now. The dominant metaphor for faith in Scripture is that of a journey. The process has as much value as the outcome as God invites us, one opportunity for generosity at a time, to seek Him. Our calling is to continually take the next step in a spiritual journey (i.e., A to B, B to C . . . but never C to Q). The journey Christ often spoke of involved movement—to the next step—but never to a static relationship. A common tendency (and concern) is that people in the church simply "get saved" and quit taking those next steps. There's no idea of "spiritual arrival" in Scripture, however. Just because we can tithe 10 percent of our income doesn't mean God will not invite us to share more than that. Just because we make it to church doesn't mean God's done feeding us with His Word. Just because our term is up after we've served on the board or as a small-group leader or youth worker doesn't mean God doesn't want to use our experience and influence to benefit others. Jesus meets us where we're at and invites us to the next step. We don't have to have the whole journey all figured out to make that next leg of the trip. Our challenge is to keep praying and seeking where God is leading us. So the question we face weekly, if not daily, is *What is my next step?*

FINDING OUR YES

The strategy in a rhythm of generosity is to figure out where we're most compelled to respond, then invest there faithfully. Proactive and systematic giving allows us to say no to other worthy causes because we've already said yes to another. (Saying yes to one thing doesn't limit opportunity, but it does give us the confidence to say no to another). I don't recommend giving to every person who asks. Sometimes I feel a prompting that I should. But if we've already prayed through our giving and are fully invested in Kingdom-on-earth initiatives and people, we don't have to feel obligated to help. We're already working off a strategy.

Giving reflects belief and support. Selfless and sacrificial giving is also one of the most formative tools in shaping us into who we want to become. In giving systematically, we resist the feeling of scarcity that can limit the potential for impact. Giving always requires faith in how God will use the gift and supply for our needs. As growing disciples, we seek to share affection, enthusiasm, empathy, or financial resources with one another. Practicing generosity requires us to demonstrate concern for others in practical ways and trust God for results.

DISCUSSION QUESTIONS

1. Who is the most generous person you know who doesn't have a considerable net worth?

2. What limits your generosity even when it would be giving for a good cause?

3. Since most of us don't like feeling indebted to someone, how do you think we can repay others' generosity? For that matter, how do you repay a gift?

4. Beyond your net worth, bank accounts, stocks, or possessions, describe how rich you are. What are some tangible signs of God's abundance in your life?

5. Based on this chapter, how would you explain the difference between a tithe and an offering to someone who might become your apprentice?

6. We have all been given gifts we can share with others. In what ways can you try to give where giving is its own reward?

7. Do you think generosity is more about the extent of the gift (of time, money, attention, etc.) or the sacrifice involved? Why?

Finding Your Rhythm

Expressing Faith through Giving

THE BOOK OF DEUTERONOMY gives us a clear picture of how to practice generosity, specifically how those who have should respond to those in need. *Deuteronomy* means "second law." The book is not introducing something new. Instead, it's a reminder of the covenant and promise of God. After forty years in the desert, Moses reminds the people about all God had done for them, the laws they must continue to obey, and the command to teach their children to love and obey God. Deuteronomy responds to two questions: (1) *How has God led us?* and, looking forward, (2) *Where does God want to take us?* For the Israelites, remembering their covenant with God meant choosing to act with compassion and generosity toward others. And as modern Christ followers, we remember our calling in the same way.

STEWARDING OUR GIFTS (AND OUR HEARTS)
Read Deuteronomy 24:10-22 and consider the following questions.

1. In this passage, who were the most vulnerable people in society? To whom might you apply this passage today?

Notice the "cost" of compassion and generosity. If you owned a field, Scripture commanded you not to harvest to the edges. The idea was to help others survive rather than to maximize your profit. Back then (and to some extent now), the people of God were God's welfare and Social Security plans. The idea isn't to solve a problem or eradicate an issue. The point is to be part of God's redemption and restoration, healing, and help. So we simply make available what we do have: a dollar, our time, a favor, a conversation, a relationship, a prayer, a significant gift, a guest room, or a cold drink. *Giving starts with seeing a need and looking to be part of a response—even if it doesn't solve anything.*

2. Why does God repeatedly remind the Israelites of their past captivity and enslavement?

As we've learned, faith is expressed in systematic or disciplined giving. Our money needs to be managed and allocated—even before God—if we are to be successful stewards. Call it financial health. It's through giving that we assume responsibility for the vision, values, and needs of a community. We're a part of God's plan to meet needs, share life, and author hope. Having a rhythm of generosity reminds us that everything we have is a gift from God—not just for our personal use but also for us to bless others with.

Stewardship starts with discipline and becomes a habit. As it does, and we align with God's heart for our lives, giving becomes a new normal, even enjoyable. Being a "cheerful giver" (2 Corinthians 9:7) isn't just about meeting others' needs. It's also about growing in our faith that God will continue to provide for us.

PRAYING FOR A POSTURE OF GENEROSITY

Find a quiet place and write a prayer of generosity. Don't rush. Include the following components in your prayer and reflection time.

- *Ask God what is keeping you from bearing more fruit.* You need a word from God about your neighbors, job, marriage, children, that friend whose life is spiraling down . . . ask whatever you wish with faith, and it will be given to you (Matthew 7:7-8).

- *Ask God what in your life needs pruning.*

- Begin with *Lord, I see . . .*, expressing gratitude for His abundant provision. You might even ask God to give you eyes to see His provision more fully.

- Then include *Lord, help me . . .*, and wait for God to prompt you on how to practice biblical stewardship and increasing generosity.

ESTABLISHING A RHYTHM OF GENEROSITY

Here are some suggestions for actions to take with a disciple, apprentice, small group, your family, or your spouse. **Choose at least one suggestion to experiment with how you might trust God more in your own life over the next month.**

- Create a plan to start systematically giving to the church. Even if you have to start with 3 percent of your income, it's a good first step. Now begin imagining and discussing a plan to increase your giving by faith. If you're giving 10 percent, ask the Lord to reveal needs and opportunities that He wants to use your gifts toward to make a difference and grow in faith.

- Find items of value that you don't use (e.g., winter clothing, warm blankets, an insulated water bottle) and *personally* redistribute them to individuals in need or local organizations that serve people in need (refugee services, the Salvation Army, etc.).

- Give to someone anonymously this week. Let the act of giving to the Lord be its own reward (i.e., leave a bag of groceries on a doorstep or a thoughtful treat on a coworker's desk, add another hour to an expired parking meter, buy a cup of coffee for a stranger in line behind you). Try this practice weekly for a month. Make it part of your prayers.

- Take a Saturday morning and learn the name of at least one homeless person in your community. Bring a bag of socks, granola bars, breakfast tacos, or Ramen noodles (these can be cooked at a fast-food restaurant; many have hot water available for such a use); a rain poncho; a coat; a hat; and a thermos of coffee with cups. Ask their name, if they'd like a cup of coffee, and the question *What's one thing you've accomplished or are good at that most people don't know?*

- Help someone (like a new neighbor or coworker) pack (or unpack) or move. Enlist a small group of friends as support.

THE RHYTHM OF GRATITUDE

Understanding How Postures and the Names of God Align Our Hearts

[David said,] "I will celebrate before the LORD.
I will become even more undignified than this,
and I will be humiliated in my own eyes."

2 SAMUEL 6:21-22

ONE DAY ON A MORNING RUN through my neighborhood, I caught a very distinct smell of spring: fresh, blooming lavender. There are two places it occurs on my six-mile run: within the first quarter mile and again at the halfway point. Each time, it is a pleasant encounter. I always like to breathe deeply and enjoy myself as if God is meeting me. But on this day, at this point in my run, as I started up a steep hill in the central Texas humidity, I caught up to a hideous, slow-crawling garbage truck. Obviously, I couldn't hold my breath long enough or speed up the hill to get by. Instead, I was left to sadly pace myself along with this noisy, stinking reminder of the mess that humanity has created. It's not that my neighbors are viler than me. The trash collector had already been to my house! I was left smiling at the realization that God creates beauty, yet we humans live with so much waste and decay of our own making. And if we end up waiting for everything to be right, better, or brighter, we will miss the good already in our lives.

With all of life's challenges, we have to recognize that gratitude is often more a discipline than a knee-jerk response. In times of plenty or times of need, in sickness and in health, gratitude is like a muscle in need of exercise.

The rhythm of gratitude includes learning God's character, offering Him praise, and declaring God's faithfulness. So how do we express God's worth amid life's mundane, fun, or challenging parts? In a culture full of diverse, shocking news headlines and a tragic pattern of doomscrolling through unfiltered social-media opinions, gratitude doesn't seem like a normal response. Christian discipleship can offer a radically different and needed narrative. Kids must learn to say "thank you" in certain situations. Similarly, we all need someone further along who can help recalibrate the posture of our hearts and provide their witness as to how they have experienced God in the most personal ways.

THE PHYSICALITY OF WORSHIP

Imagine greeting a family member without a hug, handshake, or smile. Your lack of enthusiasm would reveal a great deal about how you felt—or didn't feel—about that relative. Imagine your favorite team in your favorite sport winning the game. Enthusiasm would be the most natural reaction, and it would likely be expressed in tangible ways: cheering, clapping, or jumping up and down. Imagine experiencing an immeasurable gift of friendship and then learning that your friend is moving away. The sense of loss would be palpable. A physical reaction to the news would be impossible to hide. The point is that our physical expressions matter, and they are a significant part of how we worship God.

Worship is not always demonstrative, but the substance of worship can help us tune in to the reality of God. The word *enthusiasm* comes from the Greek words *en*, meaning "in" or "within," and *theos*, meaning "God."[1] So enthusiastic worship, on some level, is a demonstration of God within every believer.

When we talk about a rhythm of gratitude, it begins with a level of enthusiasm in declaring God's worth. And worship is intertwined with the posture of our hearts. The Hebrew idea of worship was to be thought of as perpetual service. It was understood that there were to be daily sacrifices, regular breaking of bread together, and irregular offerings for peacemaking, sin, and firstfruits of harvest.[2] In other words, worship was not a service we merely attend and evaluate, like a concert or a restaurant; it was not something to be consumed. It was more like an offering you bring, like a spiritual practice. A good example of this in the Bible is when King David lets loose with gratitude in a familiar passage (2 Samuel 6:12-15). He is abandoned, unashamed, and focused solely on the Lord's gracious love and provision. David reveals that gratitude is a natural overflow of a thankful heart as it reflects our attitude toward God. And as we'll see, gratitude naturally assumes an actual and sometimes disciplined physical response. Engaging our hearts, minds, and bodies can recenter us on the goodness of God. With a heart full of praise and adoration, David loses himself in the moment. I don't think this is a premeditated move. True worship never is. True worship is simply about you and your Lord. As David writes: "I will celebrate before the LORD. I will become even more undignified than this, and I will be humiliated in my own eyes" (2 Samuel 6:21-22).

It's interesting to think about what is worshipful about David's reaction. In some church traditions, this kind of response would be unacceptable, which is what it is to David's wife, as she makes clear in 2 Samuel 6:20. But worship overflows from within, like any expression of love and gratitude. So how do physical posture and activity connect us with God when we worship? This "undignified" passage provides a snapshot of how God's Spirit connects, aligns, and inhabits our physical response. In the verses below, notice the physical posture or response and how it helps us honor, connect with, or respond to God.

Clap your hands, all you nations; shout to God with cries of joy. (Psalm 47:1)	Clapping can be a joyful noise, even if it's off the beat! Think of your body as an instrument, and know that you've been created to declare God's worth. Do you think God is rolling His eyes at your celebration or rhythm? Why do you give applause at a concert?
They will keep my name holy; they will acknowledge the holiness of the Holy One of Jacob, and will stand in awe of the God of Israel. (Isaiah 29:23)	Standing is an act of reverence and respect. It's why we stand when a bride walks down the aisle or rise when a judge enters the courtroom.

My lips will shout for joy
when I sing praises to
You;
And my soul, which You
have redeemed.
(Psalm 71:22-23, NASB)

I will be glad and rejoice
in you;
I will sing the praises
of your name,
O Most High.
(Psalm 9:2)

Let them praise his name with
dancing.
(Psalm 149:3)

I will praise you as long as
I live,
and in your name I will
lift up my hands.
(Psalm 63:4)

Lift up your hands in the
sanctuary
and praise the LORD.
(Psalm 134:2)

Moses bowed to the ground
at once and worshiped.
(Exodus 34:8)

He [Jesus] went a little
beyond them, and fell
on his face and prayed.
(Matthew 26:39, NASB)

Unlike a tantrum, shouts of joy are as exuberant as a winning touchdown. It's unbridled enthusiasm, primarily as we identify, experience, and find our lives in Christ.

Singing invites gratitude that is expressive and declarative. Ever notice how music changes not only the feel of a room but the mood of the people as well?

Movement allows our body to become an instrument (i.e., performance art).

Lifted hands reflect an attitude of surrender, praise, or offering.

Bowing and kneeling invite us into submission as we humble ourselves before the Lord and honor Him.

Lying prostrate, particularly in prayer, demonstrates surrender and reverence. It reminds us of God's positional authority over us.

BLESS THE LORD?

In Psalm 103, David reminds himself to "bless the LORD" (verses 1, 2, 20-22, NASB). This may sound strange because it seems that God should be the one doing the blessing. However, the Hebrew word *barak* ("to bless") reveals the idea behind this custom. The word is related to the word *berek* (meaning "knee"), and the verb can also mean "to kneel." The idea is that when we bless God, we mentally bow on our knees to worship Him, acknowledging Him as the Source of all blessings. Like many Hebrew words with broad definitions, the same word is used when we thank God and when He blesses us with good things.

This story may help paint a picture. Out of the blue, my mom got a call from an old family friend. "Torunn, this is Keith Anderson," he said. They'd been friends for more than seventy years; indeed, they had been family friends since before they immigrated from Norway after World War II. Mom had served as maid of honor when Keith and Edith married. Edith was now in memory care at an assisted living facility, and Keith's heart was failing; the doctor said there wasn't any more they could do. But sharing that news wasn't the primary purpose of this unexpected call.

"I wanted to call to bless you!" Keith told my mom. "The doctor says I don't have long to live, and I need to thank you for being such an amazing friend to me, my wife, and our family all our lives."

Not every day do you get a random call from someone wanting to bless you by expressing their gratitude. Mom was a bit

THE RHYTHM OF GRATITUDE | 179

stunned. What do you say, "Ummm, well . . . thanks for think-ing of me"? "Sorry, you're about to die"?

She said, "Of course, you're so welcome, Keith. But thank *you!*" It was a special call for both giver and receiver as they spent over thirty minutes recounting stories and sharing names, prais-ing God for what might've been their final conversation. It got me thinking about how critical giving and receiving gratitude is. It's genuinely one of the most life-giving practices. Certainly, timing is significant, but so are the specific words used. It stands to reason that a rhythm of gratitude is both a posture of the heart and a physical response. Paul's charge to be "always giv-ing thanks to God the Father for everything" (Ephesians 5:20) may sound impossible to us. Yet prayers of thankfulness at all times of day were part of Paul's Jewish context. Each prayer was called a "blessing," a brief prayer honoring God as the Source of every good thing. The people of God established a rhythm for gratitude even in adversity. Imagine the level of conviction and devotion such gratitude produces when blessing the Lord is normalized.

In Jesus' time, Jews would have started with "Blessed is He . . ." They blessed the Lord upon waking, thanking Him for each part of their bodies that was still functioning. And as they dressed, they praised Him by saying, "Blessed is He who clothes the naked." When the first flowers were seen on the trees in the spring, they said, "Blessed is He who did not omit anything from the world and created within its good creations and good trees for people to enjoy!" When they heard thunder, they said, "Blessed is He whose strength and power fill the world." This pervasive act of prayer kept God's presence and love continually on their minds.[3]

Here's a great line from an Elizabeth Barrett Browning prose novel: "Earth's crammed with heaven, / And every common bush afire with God: / But only he who sees, takes off his shoes."[4] The world would have us believe that what is hard is bad and what's easy is good. But some things in life can be tough and also really good. We may never want to relive those times, but God has redeemed or shaped us through them. Like us, ancient Hebrews had blessings for the highs and lows in life. When they celebrated some long-awaited happy event, they said, "Blessed is He who has allowed us to live, sustained us, and enabled us to reach this day." Even in times of grief, they blessed God. They said, "Blessed is He who is the true judge." Uttering such blessings was a reminder that God was still good, even when they heard about tragic events, and that He will ultimately bring justice even where it doesn't seem to be present. Although Paul's words that we should always give thanks may seem extreme, many people have found that practicing these prayers of blessing can change their inner attitude. Constant gratitude to God reminds us that the world is saturated with His presence and that we are under His care.[5]

In the parable of the ten lepers (Luke 17:11-19), Jesus illustrated the nature of gratitude and the need for thankfulness. All ten were healed, but only one bothered to return to give thanks. And the one who returned was a Samaritan, while the rest were Israelites. These two groups hated each other, but these ten were forced together because of their stigmatized disease. Samaritans were thought of as "half-breeds" and not considered true children of God. Yet to make a point, the story is slanted in favor of the one who's grateful. In difficult times, it is hard to see what God is doing. On hearing some tragic news, certain rabbis had an interesting and wise but difficult saying: "Gam zu l'tovah"— "Even this is for the good."

Recently, I sat with my dad, who was struggling to find words to name his favorite Giants' player, milkshake flavor, or simply his phone. After a stroke less than two weeks earlier, he was rehabbing with a full day of speech, respiratory, and physical and occupational therapies. Maybe the most challenging part was not just seeing him lethargic and confused but also not knowing his long-term recovery prognosis.

I felt helpless, but I thought the least I could do was get him cleaned up with a shave. In my parents' sixty years of marriage, mom had never seen dad with any facial stubble. As I held his skin, I remember him teaching me to shave. Life felt like it had come full circle as he sat there pleased and content. He's never been one to be idle, much less to ask for help. So this exchange felt privileged, sort of intimate, and kind of sacred. It helped me feel present with my sadness, concern, and love. "Gam zu l'tovah" is a statement of faith in God—that even in the worst times, we know that a loving God works everything for good (Romans 8:28). Sometimes the good isn't readily apparent. Other times good feels like effort: a closed door, a bout with anxiety, or a strained marriage. But God is good, which implies that He can redeem all things in ways we can't imagine. What if every circumstance is another reason to draw near to Him?

What do we do when we know God is good and He is present and loves us, yet our circumstances overwhelm us? It's natural to feel distant; offering praise feels like work. The truth of who God is and the physical activity of worship can be a helpful way to align our hearts and minds with God's Spirit. In the parable of the ten lepers, we learn that God expects us to show gratitude. This story illustrates that gratitude pleases and connects us with the Lord, even if it requires extra effort. Indeed, all ten lepers were probably grateful, but only one came to express it: the lowly, despised Samaritan. Jesus thought this odd. I'm sure the other Jewish lepers couldn't have been happier to be healed, but they didn't voice their appreciation. If we end up waiting for everything to be better or brighter in our lives, we will miss God's good presence and faithfulness in our present and past.

The apostle Paul wrote to the Colossian church, saying,

> Let the peace of Christ rule in your hearts, since as members of one body you were called to peace. And be thankful. Let the message of Christ dwell among you richly as you teach and admonish one another with all wisdom through psalms, hymns, and songs from the Spirit, singing to God with gratitude in your hearts.
> COLOSSIANS 3:15-16

We can also often develop a bad habit of making assumptions about what others know instead of expressing ourselves in our closest relationships. We may think, *She knows I love her . . .*, *He knows I appreciate him . . .*, or *She knows I'm thankful for all she does.* The same can be true of God. We can cultivate intimacy by being intentional with our praise and thanks. Gratitude is a healthy expression but one that requires some discipline. It's a good rhythm to practice whether we feel like it or not. When we learn to express gratitude consistently, it shapes us from the inside out.

The rhythm of gratitude has two key components. First, it involves considering how our physical posture helps us express affection to God. In other words, love and intimacy go hand in hand with some kind of physicality. Second, it involves deepening our understanding of who God is by examining the names of God. As we walk with God, calling Him by His names, we can increasingly identify the character and nature of God, who is worthy of our praise.

ALIGNING OUR BODIES WITH OUR HEARTS

Try as we might, we cannot compartmentalize our lives. If we're emotionally sad, we become physically tired. If we're in a rush, we often fail to be gracious. If we feel mentally exhausted or stressed, we tend to have smaller margins for patience, care, or thankfulness. We realize that we simply cannot separate our spiritual lives from the emotional, physical, and mental aspects of our lives. Practicing gratitude makes a profound difference by readjusting our attitude, dulling our edges, and realigning our hearts with the heart of our good Father. God's Spirit works through all these aspects so that we might experience growing intimacy with the Lord.

In the following list, identify which disciplines feel most accessible to you and which ones you most resist. For the latter, try to discern what the barrier could be.

- *Gratitude assumes a physical response (2 Samuel 6; Luke 17:11-19).* Genuine praise produces a physical reaction, whether it's because of a fantastic performance, a winning touchdown, some good news, or a met need. When we talk about worship, our physical response reveals the affection in our hearts and the praise on our lips. In 2 Samuel 6, David couldn't contain his love for God. Worship is never an end in itself. Instead, true worship reveals our gratitude, surrender, devotion, need, and love for God.

- *Gratitude reminds us that God is the Source . . . that even our effort is a gift (John 15).* It's natural to think that we deserve what we've received. It's a sign of good character (and sometimes good fortune) to take advantage of opportunities. Most people work hard to build a résumé that leads to success. Yet how is it that you were born into a country that grants you certain inalienable rights? Education remains a privilege, even if it is mandatory. Literacy, clean drinking water, basic health care, living on more than two dollars a day, the ability to breathe . . . it's all a gift. While God calls us to be good stewards of what we've been given, ultimately, God remains the Source.

- *Gratitude is a spiritual muscle that needs exercise (Psalm 71).* The more we sing, recite, learn, and pray about the faithfulness of God, the more we condition ourselves toward gratitude. An excellent example is when Jesus went into the desert to endure tempting by the devil (Matthew 4).

The humanity of Christ was on full display, yet even in weakness, Jesus resisted. The strength to stand firm against temptation was rooted in Jesus' devotion to His heavenly Father. Jesus had prepared for this moment in how He had conditioned His heart, mind, and body.

- *Gratitude can be a choice despite circumstances (2 Samuel 12).* Gratitude doesn't alleviate pain. Growth requires an effort that makes us uncomfortable. At our lowest moments, it's crucial to distinguish how we feel and what is true about God. It's normal to feel God is silent, absent, or ambivalent about our circumstances. At times like these, we can reflect on what we know is true about God's character, nature, and attributes. He infinitely cares, loves, is present, rejoices, and grieves with us.

CALLING ON THE NAME(S) OF GOD

I asked a well-traveled friend about the difference between two worship leaders. He knew both personally as friends and agreed both were very competent. But only one of these leaders had achieved international recognition and broad appeal. I wondered whether this was a case of knowing the right people, pure talent, or special favor. Referring to the success of the one, my insightful friend said, "He just has a bigger thesaurus." In other words, his ability to call on God's names produced a greater intimacy. One of life's significant challenges is trying to put words to what we feel on a deep level. Knowing the names of God helps us recognize God in both beauty and sorrow and helps us find words to express both praise and petition.

Once, after a worship service ended, Neil came up with a wide-eyed, serious face, saying, "Dave, I . . . we need to talk to you!" Before I could even inquire, he stated, "Kim's pregnant. This is not what we wanted."[6]

I knew immediately what he was thinking. The past couple of years had been rough on Neil and Kim—they'd faced a difficult birth with their third child, physical health issues, unemployment, the sale of their home, downsizing their economic footprint, and the added strains of these things on their marriage. I understood the pressure they felt and what they were considering. Two days later, we met for an emotional two-and-a-half-hour lunch. Overwhelmed and conflicted, they couldn't imagine absorbing another child's financial and emotional weight. As I listened, I was reminded of the faithfulness of God. I didn't belittle anything they said, nor did I make a biblical argument for the sanctity of life.

Instead, I reminded them of their real-estate friend who specialized in renegotiating bank loans and who had saved them from foreclosure. They never filed for bankruptcy and had always had their medical needs provided for. They'd been part of a couples mentoring group in which they found great encouragement and support. But now all they could focus on was their desperate, overwhelmed response to an unplanned fourth child. I gently challenged them to remember God's daily bread all along the way. They knew God as Deliverer, Refuge, Provider, Healer, and Comforter. None of which they disagreed with. "If you agree that God is faithful and loving," I asked them, "why would He stop being any of those things now?"

Ultimately, we prayed, hugged, and went our separate ways.

I couldn't force their decision, but I committed to praying for wisdom. And what came from speaking the names of God was a new life. Nine months later, they added a beautiful, healthy girl to their home. And God has continued to reveal Himself to and provide for their family.

THE BREAD OF LIFE

In the Lord's Prayer, the line "Give us this day our daily bread" can be seen as both a request and a challenge. Can we recognize the daily bread God provides? We trust not in our pantry, our savings, our charm, or our smarts. Not in our looks or our seniority. We trust God to be our portion, our daily bread. We're more likely to walk with gratitude if we identify daily provision. A rhythm of gratitude comes from our ability to recognize the presence of God in our everyday, busy, distracted, and challenging lives.

After God delivered the Israelites from slavery in Egypt and they got to the other side of the parted Red Sea, they quickly looked around and said, "Now what are we going to eat?" The liberation from slavery felt short-lived. So God provided manna (along with some quail for protein), their literal daily bread. It was given with one instruction: Gather only enough for that day. There would be no stockpiling or hoarding. In His infinite wisdom, God said, "Take enough for today." Manna wasn't the bread they were accustomed to eating, nor was it part of their diet in Egypt. It was God providing something entirely new. The Hebrew word for *manna* (*man*) literally translates into a question: "What is it?"[7] In essence, God provided the Israelites with a question to digest each day as they learned to orient their lives around Him.

Despite living with daily provision, the Israelites constantly complained. Sometimes we, too, are tempted to be ungrateful, to think we don't have enough or that we should have more. But as we encounter undeserved gifts and significant obstacles, pure joy and daily challenges, God promises daily provision and invites us to ask, "What is it?" God doesn't want us to become so comfortable or complacent that we quit humbly seeking provision from the trusted Source. Ultimately, Jesus answered the question *What is it?* when He identified Himself as "the bread of life" (John 6:35). Do we have an ever-increasing appetite for this daily provision, our present-day manna from heaven?

THE OBJECT OF OUR WORSHIP

If we're not careful, we can quickly become the object of our own worship. Many modern worship songs are written about our subjective experiences of God rather than about our objective God. While it isn't wrong to express how we lovingly feel toward God, we need to be thoughtful about keeping God as the object of our praise, not merely the fleeting desire or intention of our praise. Regardless of our circumstances, God's character is steadfast and unchanging.

As related earlier, my church's experience with Burmese refugees has provided stories that linger. Our visits have become personal. On a Monday evening, eight of us revisited the home of a young mom from Myanmar who had recently died of cancer. She left behind a husband and three kids, ages twelve, eight, and six. He had quit his factory job two months earlier to care for his terminally ill wife. We showed up with a bowl of fresh fruit, cards with a bit of money to help with funeral expenses, and a desire to comfort. When immigrants struggle to assimilate, it's often partly because they don't have any American friends. Overwhelmed in a new culture, they often face a higher cost of living and a language barrier. It's natural to crave the familiar, which feels like home. Thankfully, we were not only familiar faces but also could stand together as brothers and sisters in Christ—an experience that blessed us all.

During our visit, the apartment began to fill with other Burmese people. The family's extended community showed up each night that week in solidarity to pay their respects and to grieve and pray together. I can only describe our prayer time as a vibrant, full-participation concert of prayer. It was a chorus of agreement, calling on the names of the Lord . . . through tears, but with hope and unwavering faith. It wasn't easy, but it was good! This happens when Sunday school leaves the classroom and becomes an exercise in humility, community, and hope. We can't simply wait for people to show up to our parties, worship services, and small-group meetings. We are sent people who can and are called by God to—bring the church to others!

When we develop a rhythm of gratitude, difficult circumstances won't deter us from belief or devotion. We gather with postures of surrender, dependency, and mutual support because no one should grieve or struggle alone. We meet to call on the name(s) of the Lord. In their grief, our Burmese friends called on the names they needed, desired, and trusted. These names were personal to the community, and it was a privilege to be part of that prayer time. They believed in what God's names reveal about His character even amid their loss. Growing in worship happens as we learn God's character, attributes, and being. Worship need not be to an anonymous entity but can flow from a personal, intimate relationship with our Creator. We see an example of this in Psalm 116:

> The cords of death entangled me,
>> the anguish of the grave came over me;
>> I was overcome by distress and sorrow.
> Then I called on the name of the LORD:
>> "LORD, save me!"
> The LORD is gracious and righteous;
>> our God is full of compassion.

PSALM 116:3-5

DISCUSSION QUESTIONS

1. How did you grow up worshiping God?

2. What attributes would you use to describe God based on your personal experience with Him?

3. In what way is worship underwhelming or uncomfortable?

4. Can you articulate two or three ways that Christ is making or has made a difference in you? How has your heart been softened, strengthened, or enlarged for a particular population or issue?

5. What does it mean to worship "in the Spirit and in truth" (John 4:24)? How has your understanding or expression of worship changed over time?

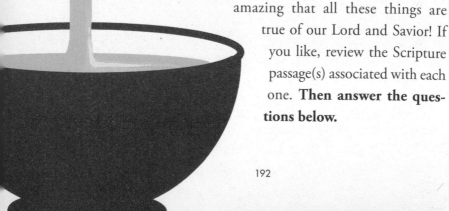

Finding Your Rhythm

Calling on the Names of God:
Understanding God's Character

PRAISING GOD HELPS US KNOW GOD. Specifically, we need to know God's names because they reveal God's character and nature. They describe unchanging truths about who God is and help ground us in truth even when circumstances cause us to question whether God is truly for us. What we find is that God is worthy of our praise!

REFLECTING ON THE NAMES OF GOD
Read through the following list of names for God. Take time to think about the implications of each name—it's amazing that all these things are true of our Lord and Savior! If you like, review the Scripture passage(s) associated with each one. **Then answer the questions below.**

Advocate (1 John 2:1)

Chief Shepherd (1 Peter 5:4)

Deliverer (Romans 11:26)

Father of Compassion
(2 Corinthians 1:3)

God Full of Compassion
(Psalm 86:15, NKJV)

God of All Comfort
(2 Corinthians 1:3)

God of All Grace (1 Peter 5:10)

God of Hope (Romans 15:13)

God of Patience and Comfort
(Romans 15:5, NKJV)

Image of the Invisible God
(Colossians 1:15)

Immanuel ("God with us";
Matthew 1:23)

Our Healer (Exodus 15:26)

Life-Giving Spirit
(1 Corinthians 15:45)

Light of the World (John 8:12)

Mediator (1 Timothy 2:5;
Hebrews 12:24)

My Fortress (Psalm 18:2)

My Glory (Psalm 3:3)

My Helper (Hebrews 13:6)

My Hope (Psalm 71:5;
1 Timothy 1:1)

My Portion (Psalm 73:26;
119:57)

My Savior (Psalm 38:22)

My Strength and My Defense
(Isaiah 12:2)

One Who Refreshes
(Psalm 23:3)

Our Potter (Isaiah 64:8)

Our Provider (Genesis 22:14)

Physician (Exodus 15:26)

Pioneer and Perfecter of Faith
(Hebrews 12:2)

Prince of Peace (Isaiah 9:6)

Redeemer (Isaiah 59:20)

Refiner and Purifier
(Malachi 3:3)

Resting Place (Jeremiah 50:6)

Resurrection and the Life
(John 11:25)

Righteous Judge (2 Timothy 4:8)

Righteous Savior
(Jeremiah 23:6)

Shelter from the Storm
(Isaiah 25:4)

Shepherd (Genesis 49:24;
Psalm 80:1)

Shield (Deuteronomy 33:29;
2 Samuel 22:31)

Source of Eternal Salvation
(Hebrews 5:9)

Spirit of Justice (Isaiah 28:6)

The Way, the Truth, the Life
(John 14:6)

Wisdom (Proverbs 8:12;
1 Corinthians 1:30)

Wonderful Counselor
(Isaiah 9:6)

Your Redeemer (Isaiah 43:14)

1. Which of these names of God have you personally experienced? As you list them, try to connect the name of God with an event or season of life where God revealed His presence.

   •

   •

   •

   •

2. Are there any names that you need help to experience or are skeptical about?

3. Which names are surprising or confusing to you? Why?

How can studying this list inform or affect your worship? Hopefully, it grows your awareness of God and hope in the promises of God. Similar to the way a thesaurus can expand your vocabulary, the names of God can help put words to how you sense and call on God. *God will always be consistent with His divine character, so the more we know of Him, the more realistic our prayers and expectations will be.*

To help you better understand the difference Christ is making in you, **add a fourth category to your timeline from chapter 1.** Try to discern God's faithfulness in the sequence of your life. Which names of God can you see during its various seasons and events? Write them down on the timeline.

PRACTICING POSTURES OF WORSHIP

Let's revisit the 2 Samuel 6 account of David dancing an undignified jig before the Lord and the whole city of Jerusalem. As we can see from David's example, gratitude is a response toward God. Like any relationship, intimacy with God can be nurtured over time, but gratitude reminds us to be sensitive (and responsive) to the prompts of the Spirit.

Read 2 Samuel 6 each day for two weeks and write or offer a prayer. Come back to 2 Samuel 6:21-22 throughout the day as a promise. Let it be an anchor despite your responsibilities or challenges. No, seriously. Try this. Set a twice-daily phone alert with the verse on it. Write the verse on a sticky note for your dashboard or computer monitor.

> [David said,] "I will celebrate before the LORD. I will become even more undignified than this, and I will be humiliated in my own eyes."
>
> 2 SAMUEL 6:21-22

Then, begin to look for ways in which God answers your prayer. Consider how you might greet the Lord differently in prayer, worship, and study.

See if God might interrupt you with an act of compassion,

generosity, or hospitality toward someone else. Our posture for gratitude is a means to declare God's worth through our lives. In the next two weeks, find at least one opportunity to yield to God's Spirit, even if it feels inconvenient or undignified.

This week, **choose at least one of the following ideas for practicing gratitude,** and make sure you share it with a friend, spouse, parent, apprentice, or older child. Consider inviting him or her to join you.

- Learn to praise God for who He is. As a springboard, use the names of God that you've experienced. Deepen your worship by thanking God for His character, acts, and being.

- Experiment with new and different postures in prayer. If you're not used to being demonstrative or expressive in worship and prayer, begin practicing biblical postures (e.g., kneeling in reverence and submission, raising hands in surrender, or cupping your hands in offering) during times alone with God.

- Find joy in giving. Practice, if necessary. Try it anonymously with an apprentice or friend. Try random acts of kindness, small favors, and other chores as an offering to God.

- Try praying using the ACTS method for a week, slowly going through **a**doration, **c**onfession, **t**hanksgiving, and **s**upplication.

- Keep a gratitude journal for thirty days. Take the time each day to write out what was life-giving and satisfying about the day. Share it with friends.

- Fast from any complaining for one day. Note the effect it has on your attitude, health, and rest.

- Immerse yourself in the life of someone who has less than you, maybe someone with much less. Serve the homeless, refugees, or kids in foster care; visit a prison; or spend an afternoon with the elderly. See the difference it makes in your perspective of your wants, desires, ambitions, and actual needs.

8

CO-MISSIONING

Recovering God's Mission for Disciplemaking

AS A NORWEGIAN IMMIGRANT, my mom decorated our home with sentimental and unique art that reminded her of her native homeland. There were decorative plates, wooden carvings, black-and-white photos, and framed hand stitching. If you asked her about any of them, there was always a story. One significant piece was a large oil painting of a traditional Norwegian coastal landscape of a fjord with a distinct color palette for the small homes and rowboats. The artist was somewhat renowned for his work, and my cousin married into this family. While her husband did not possess his grandfather's gift, their daughter Josephine demonstrated an unusual talent early on. And so, despite the artist's own renown, even more than his paintings, his great-granddaughter was his pièce de résistance—his most significant achievement—as he cultivated the natural artist in her. He gave his young protégé a mandate: "You can't sell any of your work until you've painted one hundred paintings!"

It's hard to quantify the amount of effort it took, but it probably involved hundreds of hours—a big ask when much of her work was already so good. And yet, with each successive painting, you can see the impact of her great-grandfather's instruction. You can imagine him demonstrating lighting, shading, and depth and then handing the brush over to give her the opportunity to try. And you can hear the loving critique and feedback loop with each piece.

I appreciate the discipline of refining a natural gift. Discipline develops both the craft and the person. Are we willing to commit to the slow work of developing what we've been given? In the case of a budding young artist, it's obvious to see that you're already a cut above your peers when it comes to your craft. It's easy to imagine some initial attention and the temptation to parlay that recognition into possible revenue. It's much more difficult to submit yourself to the rigorous evaluation and delayed gratification involved in honing your craft. Yet the result will only be a better product for the artist and her art. In the case of the great-grandfather artist, it might have been easier just to enjoy the shared interest of his young protégé and not worry about painstakingly helping her develop her craft. It's common to find one's worth based on personal reputation and status and not concern yourself with nurturing potential in someone else.

Have you ever had someone speak into and develop your potential? Perhaps they saw something in you academically, athletically, artistically, or in leadership. Maybe they saw something you weren't aware of or lacked confidence in. They took time, gave opportunity, perhaps even picked you out of a crowd, and then offered valuable feedback. As I shared earlier, disciple-making moves at the speed of a relationship. So when we find someone further along who earns our trust, it can be one of the most spiritually impactful things we ever experience on earth. It's easy to be defensive if we're called out or reminded of flaws. But we all need someone to invite and inspire us to be a better version of ourselves. What's more, if we learn to become this person to others, our spiritual legacy will impact countless lives.

As we close this book, let's focus on your either identifying someone further along or inviting someone as an apprentice. Hopefully, these rhythms give you the language and some framework to become a disciplemaker. Christians sometimes forget what business we're in. Our mission is not to grow a church, services, or small groups or to build buildings or a voting bloc. Instead, our business is making disciples. And according to Jesus' last words before His ascension—"You will be my witnesses, telling people about me everywhere" (Acts 1:8, NLT)—disciples are supposed to go into the entire world discipling!

So where do we start?

GET FOUND

Typically, we think *there's strength in numbers*; *bigger is better*; and *the more, the merrier*, but . . . studies show that the larger a group is, the less productive it becomes.[1] In one study, researchers found what they called the social loafing effect. Participants wore blindfolds and a type of noise-canceling headphones and were asked to shout as loudly as possible. Without exception, everyone made less noise in groups compared to when they shouted alone. Their conclusion: The mere perception that you're in a group reduces people's motivation and effort.[2]

Researchers explained how social loafing *is a feedback problem*. When groups get larger, you experience less social pressure and feel less responsibility because your performance becomes difficult, even impossible, to measure within a crowd. The danger of social loafing for the church is that individual members can get lost in the crowd: When commitment is lower, it's natural to participate less, volunteer less, tithe less, and have a shallower experience of church as a result of one's half-hearted approach to membership. Yet Jesus invites us into a personal faith *and* group participation within the church. This is why small-batch disciplemaking is critical: We cannot afford to get lost in the crowd—or to let others get lost and miss out on impactful, heart-shaping change from the inside out.

All of us yearn for significance. Hopefully, we can find it apart from our possessions, reputation, titles, or net worth. We want to know that our lives will be remembered. Yet too often, we long to be generous or compassionate but end up being self-indulgent. We want to be heroic but instead settle for preservation, caution, and fear. But in Christ, eternity has already begun! And the extent we invest our lives in others will echo into eternity.

You may have heard this saying: "The church today is raising a whole generation of mules. They know how to sweat and work hard but don't know how to reproduce themselves." It's a potent metaphor. Throughout history, mules have carried supplies, plowed fields, pulled wagons, and carried people. They are sure-footed beasts of burden, yet they are sterile and typically cannot reproduce.[3] Most churches are full of mules: good, hard-working saints. They teach classes, organize activities, host small groups, work as ushers and with kids, address the physical needs of the people and the property, and do many other good works. There is just one problem: They don't know how to reproduce their faith. But apprenticing—whether on the giving or receiving end—can be the most impactful legacy-building thing we ever do.

MOVE WITHOUT THE BALL

In basketball, teams are often defined by star players. Within every team is a go-to talent scorer around whom the offense revolves. There are complementary players, role players, and coaches who all contribute too. Specific plays are drawn to isolate and create offense around that number-one scoring threat. But such a strategy doesn't always end in championships. Not every star player functions well without the ball in their hands. And not every star player makes the players around them better. The best teams have skilled players who can *move without the ball*. Even if the ball's not in their hands, they still contribute: set a screen, grab a rebound, retrieve a loose ball, get the tip in, fill a passing lane, spread the offense, get out on a break, and so on. Given ten players on the court and only one at a time with the ball, there's a critical responsibility for all members to function as a team. In other words, players can't just stand around thinking they're not involved because someone didn't call their number.

Similarly, Christians essentially don't know how to move without the ball. We don't know how to leverage faith when we don't have a job that includes disciplemaking. Instead of seeking opportunities, we often wait to be asked to participate. Instead of finding a contribution or making a commitment, Western Christians are often (tragically) reduced to faith consumers. If you're not serving on a committee, teaching a class, helping with youth, working in the nursery, welcoming guests, or ushering for Communion . . . how do you operate as a minister in intentional and ongoing ways? Or if you find yourself as one of the faithful volunteers, likely needing a break, how can you leverage your gifts, experiences, and influence for the Kingdom outside of a ministry title? The church has a lot of people simply showing up. There's a lot of standing and sitting without actively cultivating God's Kingdom missionally and generationally. Moreover, we've built the church's effectiveness on just a few people's talents and theological training.

It's time we changed that.

Whether you're a passionate believer or a hopeful skeptic, a young follower of Christ or a seasoned saint, you will continue growing in faith by "yoking your life" with someone further along and looking to bring others along with you. All of us will. This was always Jesus' plan and hope for the church. And to be "in process" is to share that process with carefully selected others. In other words, we're supposed to be yoked in covenant relationship and practice. I'm convinced the best work is creating a spiritual legacy of the reality of Christ in others!

I began this book by posing a question about the difference between an inheritance and a legacy. As you may recall, an inheritance is something we leave *for* someone, while a legacy is what we leave *in* them. Hopefully, the rhythm of apprenticing and the outworking of your faith has helped move the goal posts of Christian salvation beyond simply showing up. Small-batch disciplemaking, training the few to reach the many, is how we participate in the Kingdom of God on earth. And the word *missio*, from which we get the word *mission*, is Latin for the act of "sending."[4] In other words, our God is a missionary God. First, God sends His Son, and then His Son sends His church! The Spirit is a missionary Spirit, the sent one, sent into the world with a purpose. We're the result of God's mission in the world. And as Jesus says in John 20:21, "As the Father has sent me, I am sending you." This means that every Christian is a *sent one*! There's no such thing as an unsent Christian who does not get to participate in the eternal purposes of God in and through the church. Remember: It's not so much that the church has a mission; it's that the mission has a church.

GROWING UP WITHOUT GROWING OLD

What do you think you'll be doing when you're in the next life stage or the one after that? Ever have that feeling there's more you want to do? It's normal to want to make an impact, create a legacy, and long for greater meaning. Since we won't simply wake up one day to be generous, compassionate, or sensitive to the leading of the Holy Spirit, the answer to the *Who do I want to become?* question starts today. To understand the trajectory of our lives, we need to have a picture of our future. What can your life look like when your peak production years are over and when—if you're fortunate—you don't have to worry about monetizing your skills and abilities?

Euless "Bic" Moore was one of the greatest influences in my life. He showed me exactly how I want to grow up without growing old. He rose to lieutenant colonel in the US Army and fought three wars. After spending a year at the Pentagon, he began teaching graduate students at Auburn University. A man of deep faith and conviction, Bic and his wife, Joyce, embarked on a long road trip to visit small rural churches. They concluded that many pastors are lonely and lack meaningful, transparent friendship. It confirmed their calling, a ministry of encouragement to pastors. *But* . . . before they'd do that, the Moores thought they should become pastors themselves. So in their fifties, he resigned and enrolled in seminary. They even relocated so that Bic could attend. From there, they pastored in rural churches for several years.

When I met Bic, he was in his seventies and was just hitting his stride. He stewarded his life with purpose, experience, humility, wisdom, and a Spirit-filled heart for prayer and reconciliation. Bic avoided the seniors group at church, saying, "All they do is complain about their bunions and about the music being too loud!" Instead, he created strategic mentoring relationships with men in their twenties and thirties. As the college and careers pastor, he was a gift! And any guy who got close to him soon became deeply involved in prayer and ministry.

Bic would often show up unannounced in my office to check in, but inevitably, he'd have a thought or an idea for me . . . like a source of inspiration from the Lord. His prophetic voice always had to do with leadership and building the future of the church. He'd refer to it as "my graduate program in pastoral studies." After I moved, we stayed in contact. Our last conversation was via instant messaging (this was when we were all still using dial-up modems, in the pre-texting era). I give him a lot of credit for adapting to new technology at his age. I saved our recorded conversations and have often returned to them. And I've thought of Bic often—in starting a church, investing in disciplemaking, and writing this book. His most potent line still brings a smile to my face:

I think God wants churches to reproduce like rabbits without the inhibitions of in-laws sleeping in the next room!

That was Bic. Constantly provoking, speaking to potential, listening to the Spirit, and encouraging young leaders like me. And he never needed a title or job description to know how to invest in others. Bic left me with a picture of how to grow up without growing old. He spoke to my potential and helped me find my contribution. Even in Bic's absence, he still inspires me to leverage what I have by making similar, personal investments in others.

Now, here's the big secret hiding in plain sight: Neither Bic nor Tim before him taught me anything new. These mentors in my life showed me how to give my faith away, as Paul said to Timothy: "Entrust to reliable people who will also be qualified to teach others" (2 Timothy 2:2). These apprenticing relationships essentially allowed me to recognize the difference Christ was already making in my life.

And you, dear faithful follower, are closer to becoming a disciplemaker than you think! You might never feel ready, but you and I also will never arrive. Somewhere in the middle of the journey is where our faith becomes transformational. You already have what it takes to invest your life in community and on mission with another person. Apprenticing doesn't require a degree, a church program, or a fancy title. It only involves a little relational capital and a place to experiment with the heart of God as you live your life as a sent one. This is at the heart of following Jesus, nurturing a legacy, and participating in God's Kingdom, which is on earth as it is in heaven. My prayer is that these rhythms, metaphors, and stories help you be and become an apprenticing follower of Jesus. Will you join me and other small-batch disciplemakers in this great co-mission of God?

Finding Your Rhythm

Run to Win . . . but Don't Forget to
Pass the Baton!

HISTORY IS TRAGICALLY FULL of examples of relay runners dropping the baton. One small exchange—after all that training, all those gifts and dreams—lost. Passing the baton seems like such a small detail in light of all the preparation for a race. And yet, the exchange carries dramatic rewards and consequences. Similarly, Christian faith thrives when people in every generation understand this life-giving, heart-changing exchange of making disciples. Discipleship is more than a church-growth program, and disciples are hand-crafted in small batches, not mass produced. With each chapter, I've included sections to find your own rhythm in hopes that you would find your stride and, by faith, pass the baton. Take the time to read, respond to, and pray through this exchange.

PIECING IT TOGETHER

Looking back, how can you find God in the sequence of your life? Review your timeline again—meaningful lessons, influential relationships, difficult seasons, and great opportunities. How is God using both the hard and the good of your life as an investment in others?

Describe at least three ways Christ has made and is making a difference in your life.

-
-
-

To what extent are you responding to the prompts of the Holy Spirit to turn, either away from or toward something or someone? Can you give big and small examples over the last six to twelve months where you've turned toward or away from something or someone?

Give an example of a time you experienced a "divine interruption."

What do you think God was saying through it?

What did you do in response?

Is there a small handful of spiritually curious people with whom God has shown you favor? What kind of next steps can you suggest for your people of peace? How do you pray for them?

•

•

•

How do you experience the presence and person of the Holy Spirit? Recall the fivefold evidence of the Holy Spirit from chapter 5. Can you identify ways in which the Holy Spirit is active and growing in each area?

• Proof of a greater capacity to love:

• Example(s) of boldness in your witness:

• Evidence of finding power for obedience:

- Occurrence of verbal expression:

- Testimony of the fruit of the Spirit:

BECOMING AN APPRENTICING LEADER

As we conclude, it's essential to talk through your next steps in spiritual reproduction. In some ways, your notes in this field guide can be the beginning of lesson plans for you to lead. Take the time to do this final study. My suggestion is to do this in several sittings, not all at once. Jot down some notes and return to them several times.

> What do you think created the most significant impact for a disciple in ancient Israel: (1) knowledge from the rabbi; (2) the example of the rabbi; or (3) a relationship with the rabbi? It's really a combination of all three. But I imagine one disciple might've thrived because of the knowledge offered while another grew more because of the relationship, and still another needed a model to follow. Think of what you know of the twelve disciples. Can you make a case for three

different disciples who primarily grew because of knowledge, example, and relationship, respectively?

Now answer the previous question for yourself by ranking each of these apprenticing methods in your personal and spiritual growth.

How have your words, desires, attitudes, and motivations changed, even in some small way, since you became a Christian? In the past year? As you've gone through this book? Is there an area where you've overcome, surrendered, or experienced conviction about something?

Whom might you consider inviting into this apprenticing journey by sharing your experience going through the rhythms together? Think about a person who is active in serving others and/or in asking questions. Consider your chemistry, the proximity of your lives, and their emotional ability to be teachable. How would you structure your time together?

NOTES

INTRODUCTION

1. JR Woodward and Dan White Jr., *The Church as Movement: Starting and Sustaining Missional-Incarnational Communities* (Downers Grove, IL: IVP Books, 2016), 24. Woodward and White cite Skye Jethani and Scott Bessenecker's concept of "Christian-industrial complex," which was influenced by Dwight Eisenhower's "military-industrial complex."
2. Neil Cole, *Church 3.0: Upgrades for the Future of the Church* (San Francisco: Jossey-Bass, 2010), 47.
3. Barna, "Two in Five Christians Are Not Engaged in Discipleship," January 26, 2022, https://www.barna.com/research/christians-discipleship-community.

CHAPTER 1 | THE RHYTHM OF APPRENTICING

1. While the word translated as *commandment* in these verses is the Greek *entolē*, it has a similar meaning to the Hebrew concept of *mitzvah*, which Jesus' original audience likely would have had in mind.
2. Robert E. Coleman, *The Master Plan of Discipleship* (Grand Rapids, MI: Revell, 2020), 76.
3. An early conversation with friend and mentor Dr. Harv Powers introduced me to this developmental thread of Barnabas's life and ministry. Harv went on to expand and publish his thoughts in a book I highly recommend called *Redemptive Leadership*. His redemptive model identifies levels of leadership. The first three levels are as follows: Level 1: Competency, Level 2: Principle/ Intelligence, and Level 3: Character. If a leader is able to push through, then they can experience Level 4: Transformation (if not, they likely return to operating from the familiar base of core competencies). Level 5 is Redemptive leadership, which is where he highlights the work of Barnabas, even after his falling out with Paul. Harv Powers, *Redemptive Leadership: Unleashing Your Greatest Influence* (Littleton, CO: Illumify Media Group, 2022).

4. Jonah Sachs, *Winning the Story Wars: Why Those Who Tell—and Live—the Best Stories Will Rule the Future* (Boston: Harvard Business Review Press, 2012), 153.

CHAPTER 2 | THE RHYTHM OF RENEWAL

1. David Whyte, *Midlife and the Great Unknown* (Boulder, CO: Sounds True, 2008), Audible audio edition, 2 hours, 32 minutes.
2. Harry Emerson Fosdick, *The Meaning of Prayer* (Boston: Pilgrim Press, 1915), 87.
3. Fosdick, *The Meaning of Prayer*, 87.
4. My Jewish Learning, "Teshuvah, or Repentance," accessed May 8, 2023, https://www.myjewishlearning.com/article/repentance.

CHAPTER 3 | THE RHYTHM OF HOSPITALITY

1. The layout of the Second Temple in Jerusalem began with the largest, most exterior Court of Gentiles. Gentiles (non-Israelites) and ritually unclean Israelites were forbidden, on pain of death, from passing through its gates to the interior areas. Next was the Outer Court, or the Court of Women, where Jewish women were allowed to pray and worship. The third court was the Inner Court, reserved for Jewish men, where sacrifices would be offered. The two holiest places central to the Temple were the Holy Place, which was reserved for the priests, and the Holy of Holies, which originally held the Ark of the Covenant but was empty in the time of the Second Temple. See https://www.biblestudy.org/biblepic/interior-diagram-of-temple-in-jerusalem.html.

CHAPTER 4 | THE RHYTHM OF COMMUNITY

1. Henri Nouwen, *Bread for the Journey: A Daybook of Wisdom and Faith* (New York: HarperOne, 2006), 23.
2. Georges Florovsky, "Empire and Desert: Antinomies of Christian History," *CrossCurrents* 9, no. 3 (Summer 1959): 233.
3. As quoted in *Advent and Christmas Wisdom from Henri J. M. Nouwen*, A Redemptorist Pastoral Publication (Liguori, MO; Liguori, 2004), 44.
4. *Advent and Christmas*, 44. Transcription of a 1994 speech to members of FADICA.
5. David Eckman, *Becoming Who God Intended* (Eugene, OR: Harvest House, 2005), 163–164.
6. Emphasis added to Scripture in the list below.

CHAPTER 5 | THE RHYTHM OF COMPASSION

1. To learn more about the school, visit http://www.unitedlearningcentre.com.my/about-the-centre.

2. Blue Letter Bible, "Lexicon: Strong's H7356—*raḥam*," accessed May 8, 2023, https://www.blueletterbible.org/lexicon/h7356/kjv/wlc/0-1.

3. I'm not sure where I first encountered this from Lacoste, but I think an author I read for my doctorate program quoted it in their writing.

4. Not his real name.

5. I first heard Richard Dahlstrom, pastor of Bethany Community Church Seattle, tell this story and later familiarized myself with it. This part of the account I learned from him.

6. As recounted in Gene Getz, *The Measure of a Man: Twenty Attributes of a Godly Man* (Ventura, CA: Gospel Light Publications, 2004), 141.

7. Lois Tverberg, "Loving Your Neighbor, Who Is Like You," En-Gedi Resource Center, June 4, 2019, https://engediresourcecenter.com/2019/06/04/loving -your-neighbor-who-is-like-you-2.

8. Walter Brueggemann, *The Prophetic Imagination*, 2nd ed. (Minneapolis: Fortress Press, 2001), 88.

9. Jewish Virtual Library, "Charity (Tzedakah): Charity Throughout Jewish History," accessed May 8, 2023, https://www.jewishvirtuallibrary.org /charity-throughout-jewish-history.

10. Blue Letter Bible, "Lexicon: Strong's G3844—*para*," accessed April 14, 2023, https://www.blueletterbible.org/lexicon/g3844/kjv/tr/0-1.

11. Blue Letter Bible, "Lexicon: Strong's G2564—*kaleō*," accessed April 14, 2023, https://www.blueletterbible.org/lexicon/g2564/kjv/tr/0-1.

CHAPTER 6 | THE RHYTHM OF GENEROSITY

1. To see some of Starla's work, visit https://starlamichelle.com.

2. These questions are adapted from a blog post my friend Leonard Sweet wrote on why the concept of trusteeship is more relevant than stewardship: "Freely You Have Received, Freely Give," leonard sweet.com, accessed May 11, 2023, https://leonardsweet.com/freely -you-have-received.

3. The "trust fund baby" application in this context is from a Zoom discussion with my doctoral cohort.

4. CBS Pittsburgh, "Bride Given Away by Man Who Received Her Dad's Heart," August 6, 2016, https://www.cbsnews.com/pittsburgh/news/bride -given-away-by-man-who-received-her-dads-heart; and CBS Pittsburgh, "Man Who Received Bride's Father's Heart to Walk Her Down Aisle," August 5, 2016, https://www.cbsnews.com/pittsburgh/news/man-who -received-brides-fathers-heart-to-walk-her-down-aisle.

5. Bill Heinrich, "Imagery of Vine and Branches," Mysteries of the Messiah, December 21, 2015, https://www.mysteriesofthemessiah.net/2015/12 /15-01-01-imagery-of-vine-and-branches/#_ftn2.

6. Mike Breen and the 3DM Team, *Building a Discipling Culture: How to*

Release a Missional Movement by Discipling People Like Jesus Did, 2nd ed. (Pawleys Island, SC: 3 Dimension Ministries, 2014), 92.

7. For more on the use of Hinnom Valley at this time, see https://www.that theworldmayknow.com/jerusalems-hinnom-valley.

8. Parker J. Palmer, *Let Your Life Speak: Listening for the Voice of Vocation* (San Francisco: Jossey-Bass, 2000), 48.

CHAPTER 7 | THE RHYTHM OF GRATITUDE

1. Online Etymology Dictionary, s.v. "enthusiasm [*n.*]," accessed May 9, 2023, https://www.etymonline.com/word/enthusiasm.

2. Blue Letter Bible, "Condensed Bible Cyclopedia," accessed May 9, 2023, https://www.blueletterbible.org/search/Dictionary/viewTopic.cfm?topic =CT0000039.

3. Lois Tverberg and Bruce Okkema, *Listening to the Language of the Bible: Hearing It through Jesus' Ears* (Holland, MI: En-Gedi Resource Center, 2004), 85–86.

4. Elizabeth Barrett Browning, *Aurora Leigh*, 3rd ed. (London: Chapman & Hall, 1857), 304.

5. Tverberg and Okkema, *Listening to the Language*, 85–86.

6. Neil and Kim are not their real names.

7. Blue Letter Bible, "Lexicon: Strong's H4478—*mān*," accessed May 9, 2023, https://www.blueletterbible.org/lexicon/h4478/niv/wlc/0-1.

CHAPTER 8 | CO-MISSIONING

1. "When Gallup examined engagement by company size, it found the highest employee engagement level by far (42%) in companies with fewer than 10 people, suggesting something unique and beneficial about working in a smaller, tight-knit work environment when it comes to engagement"; Gallup, *The State of the American Workplace: Employee Engagement Insights for U.S. Business Leaders*, 2013, 31, https://www.gallup.com/services/176708 /state-american-workplace.aspx. Also see Lingfei Wu, Dashun Wang, and James A. Evans, "Large Teams Develop and Small Teams Disrupt Science and Technology," *Nature* 566 (2019): 378–82, https://doi.org/10.1038 /s41586-019-0941-9.

2. Bibb Latané, Kipling Williams, and Stephen Harkins, "Many Hands Make Light the Work: The Causes and Consequences of Social Loafing," *Journal of Personality and Social Psychology* 37, no. 6 (June 1979): 822.

3. This is partly because mules have an odd number of chromosomes from their hybrid parentage: thirty-two from the mother (a horse) and thirty-one from the father (a donkey). See https://worldanimalfoundation.org /farm-animals/mules.

4. Alan Hirsch and Lance Ford, *Fast Forward to Mission: Frameworks for a Life of Impact* (Grand Rapids, MI: Baker Books, 2011), 13.

NavPress is the book-publishing arm of The Navigators.

Since 1933, The Navigators has helped people around the world bring hope and purpose to others in college campuses, local churches, workplaces, neighborhoods, and hard-to-reach places all over the world, face-to-face and person-by-person in an approach we call Life-to-Life® discipleship. We have committed together to know Christ, make Him known, and help others do the same.®

Would you like to join this adventure of discipleship and disciplemaking?

- Take a Digital Discipleship Journey at **navigators.org/disciplemaking**.
- Get more discipleship and disciplemaking content at **thedisciplemaker.org**.
- Find your next book, Bible, or discipleship resource at **navpress.com**.

f @NavPressPublishing

🐦 @NavPress

📷 @navpressbooks

CP1790